FIANNA'S STORY

October 16, 2020

For Barney,
May this story bring you
gladness and nurture your
spirit.

Nancy L. Bieber

NANCY L. BIEBER

Fianna's Story
by Nancy L. Bieber

Library of Congress Number: 2020905281
International Standard Book Number: 978-1-60126-674-3

Masthof Press
219 Mill Road | Morgantown, PA 19543-9516
www.Masthof.com

TABLE OF CONTENTS

FIANNA'S FAMILY TREE

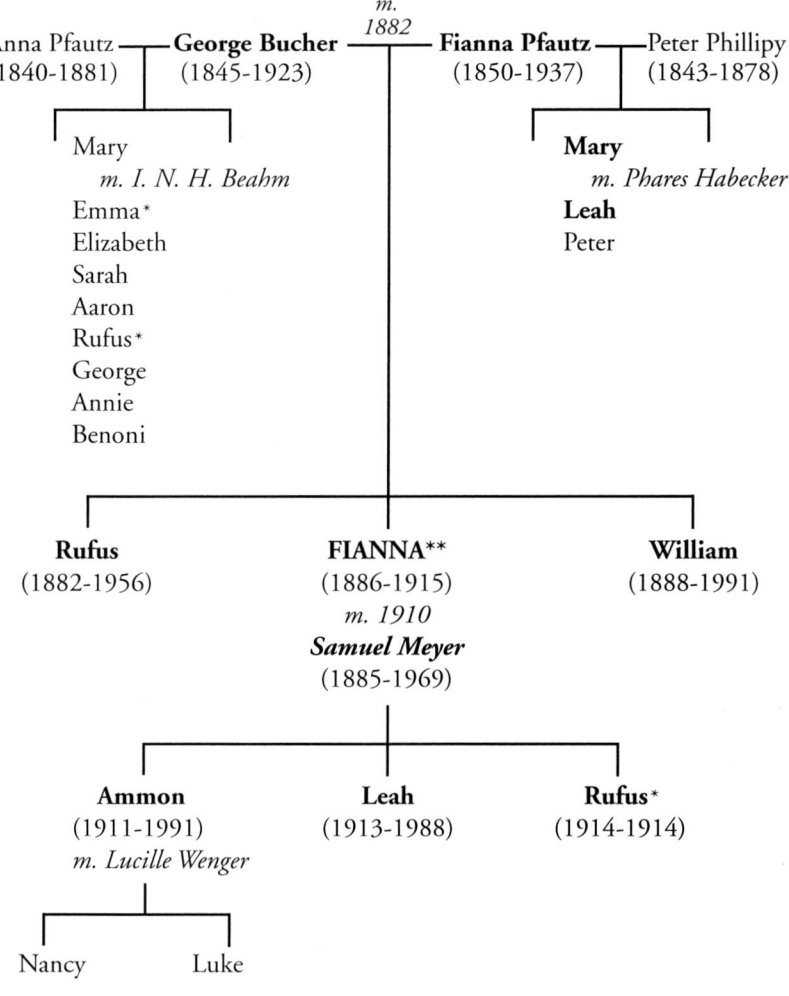

Anna Pfautz ——— **George Bucher** — *m.*
(1840-1881)   (1845-1923)   *1882*   **Fianna Pfautz** ——— Peter Phillipy
                                                    (1850-1937)   (1843-1878)

Mary
  m. I. N. H. Beahm   **Mary**
Emma*   *m. Phares Habecker*
Elizabeth   **Leah**
Sarah   Peter
Aaron
Rufus*
George
Annie
Benoni

Rufus   **FIANNA****   **William**
(1882-1956)   (1886-1915)   (1888-1991)
                           m. 1910
                           Samuel Meyer
                           (1885-1969)

Ammon   **Leah**   **Rufus***
(1911-1991)   (1913-1988)   (1914-1914)
m. Lucille Wenger

Nancy   Luke

* Died Before Adulthood
** Fianna's name was pronounced Fī-ăń-na within her family.

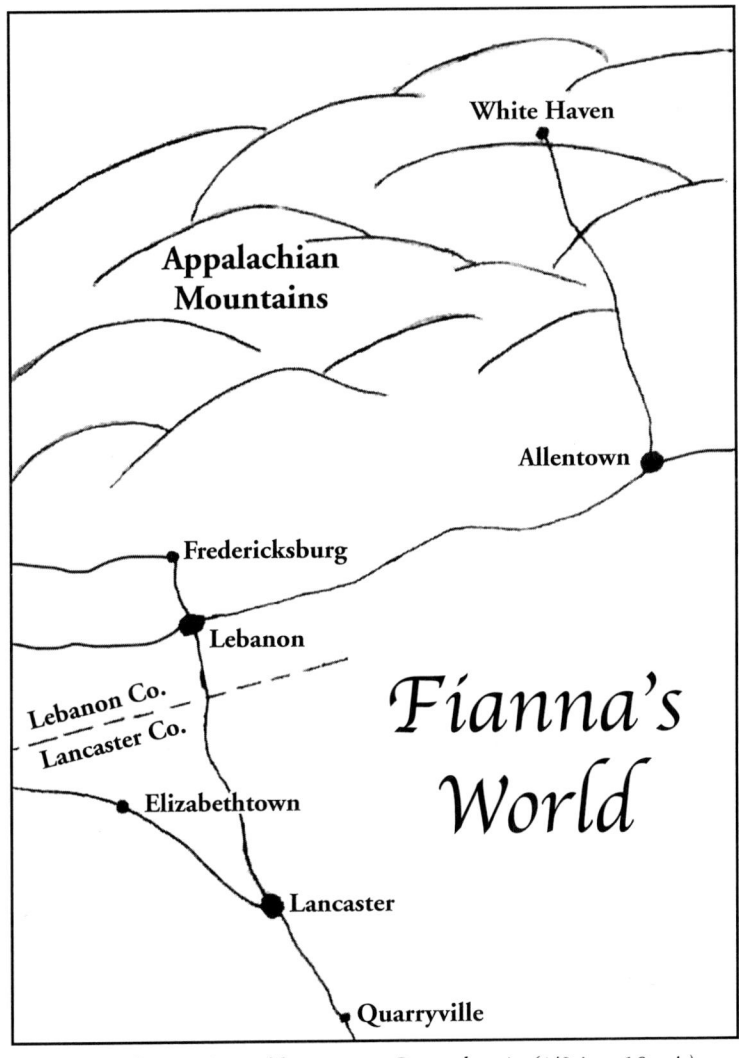

White Haven

Appalachian
Mountains

Allentown

Fredericksburg

Lebanon

Lebanon Co.
Lancaster Co.

*Fianna's
World*

Elizabethtown

Lancaster

Quarryville

Map of Fianna's world in eastern Pennsylvania (1/2 in.=10 mi.)

INTRODUCTION

Fianna Bucher Meyer was the wife of Samuel Meyer and mother of my father Ammon. Fianna was my grandmother although I never knew her. She died of tuberculosis when she was 28 years old. In 1915, the year of her death, there was no cure for this disease. Her little boy, Ammon, was not yet four, and her daughter, Leah, was two.

My father had only faint memories of his mother. He told me once that she was slender and had dark lustrous hair. I wonder if he could have remembered more if I had pressed him. I wonder how much he thought of her. I wish I had asked him.

Fianna's husband, Samuel, never forgot her. Fifty years after she died, he wrote to her sister about "this day sacred to our memory." I never asked him about her, though. I was only a child then and didn't think about such things.

Fianna's death was a family tragedy we never spoke of. But in recent years I have wondered about her. What would she have been like if she had lived? What kind of mother to Ammon as he grew? What kind of grandmother or perhaps great-grandmother? What-if questions have no answers, but the questions still persisted. I looked at her picture sitting on my desk, but she herself was a mystery.

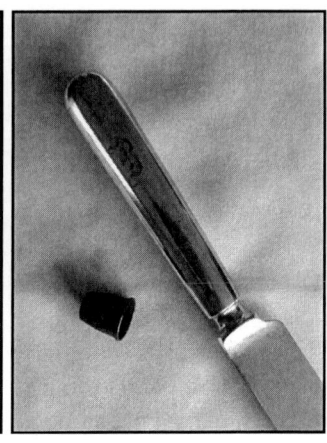

Fragment from Fianna's wedding dress   *Silver knife with* B *and Fianna's childhood thimble*

I remembered that my attic contained unopened boxes of family papers and pictures, handed down from my parents and grandparents. I decided to explore them. There I found hundreds of letters and postcards written to Fianna and by her, as well as shoeboxes filled with cherished artifacts from her life. Perhaps because she died so young, small mementoes of her life had been carefully preserved—her school report cards, a childhood dress, her thimble, and a snippet of cloth from the dress she was married in and buried in. I've seen her copybooks, filled with an evenly flowing script. I've held her watch and the silverware engraved with her initial. I even read the bill from a semester at college.

Tucked into my dusty attic was her story. A century after her death, I found the treasure I needed to begin to understand Fianna, to begin to know her life—both the joy and the tragedy of it.

This is what I discovered about my grandmother.

CHAPTER 1

THE JOURNEY

It was a cold December morning in 1914, and the new train station in Lebanon, Pennsylvania bustled with activity. Passengers crowded the ticket counter. Porters hauled trunks and mailbags. Doors to the platform opened and closed repeatedly, letting in cold gusts of air that rippled papers and waved the feathers on ladies' hats. People sitting on the waiting room benches slowly began to gather their belongings, and their friends and family prepared to say farewell.

Everyone was eagerly waiting for the arrival of the "Harrisburg Special," the important long-distance train that originated in the state capitol, puffed its way east through the mountains until it crossed the Delaware River and finally came to a halt in Jersey City.

In the midst of all this bustle, one young couple was unmoving. Samuel and Fianna Meyer turned to each other in quiet conversation, an island of stillness amid the noisy, eager excitement that surrounded them. His black suit coat buttoned up to his neck and her simple black bonnet and shawl identified them as "plain folk," belonging to one of the Brethren or Mennonite religious communities so common to this part of Pennsylvania. A well-worn suitcase and several bags lay by their feet. Their trunk had already been ticketed, and now it waited with several others on the trolley for the train to arrive.

Sitting between them was a solemn-faced little boy holding tightly to his mother's hand. Three-year-old Ammon had dark hair that fell over his forehead in bangs and big brown eyes that explored the space and people around him. He'd traveled by train before, but not from this station and never for this reason.

Finally the whistle blew; the rhythmic chugging of the train was heard. There was the smell of smoke and the squealing of brakes. Passengers poured out through the doors under the handsome octagonal tower and spread out along the platform.

The train had arrived, and it was time to go. Reluctantly, the young couple rose. He gathered up their bags and led the way. She, holding Ammon's hand, followed close behind.

Fianna and Samuel, so somber of face and dress, settled themselves and their son into their carriage. Samuel stowed the bags onto the rack above them. This young couple was married only four years, but they grew up in the same close religious community and had known each other their whole lives. Home was a farm north of Lebanon, and Samuel helped to support his family by working in a local bank.

If a passenger boarded the train at Lebanon and sat across from them, he might have smiled to see Ammon bounce on the seat as he waited for the train to start up. He might have been amused by the little boy's intent observation of the passing scenes when the train began to move.

An observant fellow traveler would also have noticed how thin and pale Fianna was and wondered about the way she held so tightly to her husband's arm. In the manner of casually-met strangers, he might have asked them where they were going on this cold December day. "To Allentown," they would have replied, "but we change trains there for White Haven."

White Haven! That explained Fianna's frail appearance. That explained the air of anxious hope and fear that clung to them even when they answered Ammon's eager questions about what he saw outside the window. Their sober manner had little to do with religion. It had everything to do with their destination: White Haven Tuberculosis Sanatorium.

Theirs was a journey of desperation, a holding on to hope because the alternative was unthinkable. Fianna had been sick for a long time. Or, as she preferred to say, she wasn't "in good health." She had lost weight and was frequently feverish, with a cough that continually got worse. She longed to care for her family and home but was too tired to do it. She and Samuel repeatedly consulted local doctors but nothing seemed to help.

Finally they'd gone to a hospital-based physician with more training and experience who confirmed what they must have secretly feared for months. Fianna had consumption. Today we call it tuberculosis. Today, although it is still a very serious diagnosis, it is curable with a long and complex course of antibiotics. Back then it was a leading cause of death, and no one knew how it spread. Some people survived tuberculosis, but many did not. There was no real cure although there were many treatments.

This winter journey was taking Fianna away from her home and family to a specialized treatment center for tuberculosis. There she would receive the best that medicine had to offer in 1914. The sanatorium sat high on a mountain ridge above the village of White Haven. The last stage of their journey would be a buggy ride up the mountain or, if the mountain was covered by snow, perhaps a sleigh ride.

This was a journey into the unknown in many ways. Fianna and Samuel had never traveled beyond south central Pennsylvania's rural farming communities and the circles of family and friendship that so strongly rooted them there. The familiar undulating hills and valleys, a patchwork of cultivated fields and meadows, would be replaced by the thick forests and steep slopes of the Appalachian Mountains of northern Pennsylvania.

What was the sanatorium like? What would it be like to live there? She was entering a community of fellow patients, many who were immigrants from the cities who spoke other languages. Who would her roommates be? What would they make of her, her plain dress, her regular prayers and Bible reading? Fianna and Samuel knew a little about the treatment she would receive. She was going to sleep outdoors and stay in bed most of the time. There would be a special diet. But what would it actually be like?

Hardest of all the unknowns was the unspoken one. What would the future bring? They knew tuberculosis killed, but it didn't kill everyone. Would the hopes Fianna and Samuel had for their life together come to nothing? Would she see little Ammon grow up?

Samuel looked at the woman he called his sweetheart, longing to take her in his arms one more time even though they were not alone. Instead he squeezed her hand again. He believed that God answered heartfelt prayer, and that God could heal. Fianna believed that, too. They also believed they needed to use all the medical means available—even if that meant sending Fianna to live at White Haven Sanatorium. They believed this treatment could strengthen her to fight off the disease. But sometimes people who went to tuberculosis sanatoriums didn't return. Sometimes prayers for healing didn't bring healing. They knew that, too.

Ammon, excited by the adventure of travel, was unburdened by their hopes and fears. He'd been told "Mamma is going away to get well," and he didn't question it. As they rode into the mountains, he squealed with delight at the snowy slopes. His parents smiled at his pleasure though their apprehension grew as they neared White Haven.

For Fianna, leaving home, the farm, family, and church community she loved, had been hard. Saying goodbye to Samuel and Ammon would be much harder.

CHAPTER 2

THE CHILD

On June 1, 1886, baby Fianna was born to George Bucher and Fianna Phillipy Bucher in Lebanon County, Pennsylvania. She was the second youngest of 14 children. A large family! Both her parents were widowed and had had children with their first spouses. George brought eight into the marriage, mother Fianna three, and they had three children together.[1]

When Fianna was born, she had two half sisters named Mary. Nineteen-year-old Mary Bucher was the oldest child in the family. When Fianna was only four, this sister married and moved to Virginia. I wonder whether Fianna understood why she left home and moved so far away. Mary had met her future husband when she was a student at Bridgewater College in Virginia, and he was a teacher there. The other Mary-sister, Mary Phillipy, married a local farmer and insurance agent. This Mary continued to be close to her little sister, helping to raise her as a child and eventually helping to raise Fianna's child when Fianna died.

Although the older children went away to school, married, and created their own homes, it was still a very full and

---

[1]   See Fianna's family tree on page iv.

lively household during these early years. The family lived on a farm in southern Lebanon County, an area of green meadows, woodlands, and rich soil for crops. Little Fianna toddled after older siblings, with perhaps much of her care being given by older sisters. She played and ran barefoot in the summertime, but she also learned to do her share of chores. On a farm there is no end to the chores, and all the children needed to help. She gathered eggs and, as she grew older, she learned to milk the cows. She helped prepare meals. She learned to sew with an older sister by her side. Among my treasures is her childhood thimble that just fits my little finger. I imagine her learning to darn socks with this thimble on her finger.

Fianna's clothing was homemade, and most of it was probably the hand-me-down variety. Received from older sisters or cousins who lived nearby, her dresses and petticoats and shawls were well worn by the time she got to wear them. A box in my attic holds a brown tweed cape sewn with beautiful small stitches that her mother made just for her. The cape has a label pinned to it that says "Mamma's cape when a girl."[2] Since she was the youngest daughter, it was never handed down to another. Her mother's father had been a professional tailor as well as a farmer. "Grandpa Pfautz" died the year Fianna was born, but perhaps special skills with needle and thread were passed on through her mother's family.

Fianna's family were leaders in the nearby Tulpehocken congregation of the German Baptist Brethren (later called Church of the Brethren). George and his brother Christian were among those

---

[2]   The note was written by Fianna's daughter Leah who was my aunt.

selected by the congregation to be ministers to the congregation. In this denomination, ministers served without pay, preaching at scattered meetinghouses on Sundays, and farming or teaching school to support their families during the week. Christian had been the minister who had married Fianna's parents.

I can picture little Fianna sitting on her mother's lap, snuggly wrapped in a shawl, as the buggy took them to church on Sunday morning where perhaps her father or Uncle Christian would preach. The children all sat with their mother, trying to be attentive and quiet during the lengthy services. I hope Fianna had a handkerchief to fold and refold or perhaps a soft toy to quietly entertain her during these long mornings. There must have been a few Sundays when a big sister was asked to take one of the littlest ones out of the service because they were just too restless.

Besides his ministry of preaching, Fianna's father had a strong interest in Christian education. It spurred him to begin a Sunday School in their church. Held on Sunday afternoon or evening, all the children and adults of the community were invited even if they weren't part of the congregation.

Sunday School was a radical innovation among the Brethren at this time, and there were those in the church who disapproved of it. However, Fianna's father, George, was a strong and determined man, and the Sunday School became a reality. Fianna and her siblings were in attendance, of course. Fianna's Sunday School attendance card for "Second Quarter 1895, Primary Department" informs me a century later that she had perfect attendance.[3]

---

[3]   This first Sunday School closed in a few years because of lack of congregational support.

When she was six, Fianna started attending public school. Holding the hand of an older sister or brother, she walked along a dusty country road to "Centre School" of Millcreek Township, the local one-room school close to their farm. Fianna's report card for her first year, 1892-93, only contains six spaces for monthly reports, suggesting that this rural school was in session for half a year. The first two months show no grades at all but after that she averaged between 75 and 85—except in "Deportment." There she received a consistent 95. This little girl had already learned to sit quietly, and she gave no trouble to an overworked teacher. Fianna was graded in reading, penmanship, and composition, and each month her grades rose a little. It was a good beginning.

		SESSION —OF— 1892-93.	Spelling.	Reading.	Penmanship.	W. Arithmetic	M. Arithmetic.	Grammar.	Geography.	History.	Physiology.	Drawing.	Composition.	Algebra.	Monthly Av.	Deportment.	Times Tardy.	Days Absent.	Days Present.
	The highest degree of excellence is denoted by 100.	1st Month.																	
		2nd "																	
		3rd "		75	75								75		75	95		5	15
		4th "		78	78								77		79	95			20
		5th "		80	82								80		81	95			19
		6th "		84	86								83		84	95			
		Av. for Term.		79	80								79		80	75			

Fianna's first report card

When Fianna was nine, the family's life was abruptly uprooted. On a preaching trip south to the city of Lancaster, father George learned that there was no German Baptist Brethren congregation in southern Lancaster County. After prayerful consideration, he decided he was called to start a church.

This decision meant the whole family would leave their farm, their church, and the nearby family. I wish I could have heard the discussions within the Bucher household during that time. What did mother Fianna think and feel? Did she object to leaving family and friends, the familiar community, and the familiar farmhouse? Did she argue with her husband—or did she understand this to be missionary work and loyally support his calling? And what about all the children? How did they feel about leaving their friends, cousins, and schoolmates? What did Fianna understand about the impending change? Was it an eagerly anticipated adventure, or did she cry as she said good-bye to her cousins?

George didn't waste any time. Within six months, he sold the old farm in Lebanon County and bought a new one near the small town of Quarryville in Lancaster County. Packing as many belongings as they could into a huge Conestoga wagon, they set off. This was not an easy journey. In March of 1896, when they moved, the roads were muddy and rutted. They traveled slowly. One account says it took two days to travel the forty miles. Relatives and church friends helped them along the way, but it was still a very challenging trip.[4]

---

[4]   *A Century of Service at the Grove, Mechanic Grove Church of the Brethren, 1897-1997.* Marie K. Bucher, 1997, p. 10.

CHAPTER 3

The Girl at School and Home

While father George was drumming up support for the fledgling church—held in the Bucher home, of course—and the older children and mother Fianna were acquainting themselves with their new home, the younger children started attending a new school. I have three monthly report cards from little Fianna's years at Prospect School. Examining them, I see that she kept her high marks (90) in deportment. Her reading, spelling and writing grades are 85-90 while arithmetic is slightly lower, 80-85. My grandmother and I are alike in this. My verbal grades have always been higher than my arithmetic grades, too.

Along with her report cards, I found two additional cards. On one side is a pretty picture of children playing. On the other side is written "Miss Annie E. Rutt to Fianna P. Bucher. Feb. 24, 1897. Headmarks." with "Prospect School. Lanc. Co." at the bottom of the card. "Headmarks" refers to the student at the head of the class. I think these special "headmarks" cards were a gift from Fianna's teacher, perhaps purchased out of her own small salary. Both these cards carry the same date, and I wonder what was special

Fianna's report card from Prospect School

Completed penmanship book

about this day. Was eleven-year-old Fianna head of the class on that day?

The most fascinating artifacts from Fianna's school years are two penmanship books. In these books, she copied the writing modeled at the top of the page again and again until she filled the page. On the cover of one book Fianna wrote, "I got this book 1897. I had to stop to go to school then. I finished it in 1898." On the other book cover is "Fianna Bucher Nov. 21, 1898" and "Dec. 15 It is finished." Fianna was twelve, and she loved practicing her penmanship. She shaped each word elegantly and smoothly with her fountain pen. As I paged through her books more than a century later, I discovered that her penmanship was indeed exquisite! I understand why she loved to write.

Among the attic treasures is a Public School Tablet with Fianna's name on the cover. It contains more evidence of her schoolwork, including math problems to solve ("How much will 5 tons of hay cost if $10 will buy 5/6 of a ton?") and sentences to diagram ("Diagram this sentence: He that hath knowledge spareth his words."). There are verbs and their tenses, vocabulary words and their meanings ("advertise—to inform, affable—easy of conversation").

The tablet even includes biology questions to answer. "What juices mix with partly digested food in the intestines and what is their action on the food? Describe the liver and give the effects of alcohol on the liver." Fianna was probably in seventh or eighth grade when she tackled these challenging questions. Even without seeing a report card from these years, I believe that she did well in school. Her parents valued education highly; doing well was expected in her family.

Fianna's grammar homework

As Fianna grew up, the house was emptying. More siblings married. Her assistance and skill with housework was increasingly needed. Growing and preserving food, sewing, cleaning, doing laundry, and caring for the chickens were all important to keep the home running. Her life was full.

Family remained important for Fianna and her parents. There were visits and shared harvests with the grown-up brothers and sisters who lived nearby. But since many relatives still lived 40 miles away in Lebanon County and some of her siblings had moved even farther away, letters rather than visits kept the family close and connected. Writing to her cousin Amy in Lebanon County when she was 18, Fianna gave news about the scattered family:

Dear Cousin and Sister Amy:-

You may not be expecting an answer from me any more but I think it is very nice to hear from our Uncles and Aunts and cousins once in a while . . . I just finished writing a letter to [older brother] Benoni, and also read over your letter. How is Uncle Christian and Aunt Eliza? . . .

It is past nine P.M. I am all alone downstairs in the sitting room. So I have plenty of room to think. [Younger brother] Willie went to bed a good while ago. [Older brother] Rufus went to Elizabethtown again. Father and mother went up to New Providence . . .

[Older sister] Lizzie has not been home for over eight years. It seems a long time and yet how short! She has two girls. [Older brother] Aaron is out there, too, in Indiana.

This morning at the table, mother said she'd like to come over and visit the aunts and uncles when the trolley is finished to Quarryville. Then father said when it is built over to Shaefferstown. That may be quite a while yet . . .

I remain,
Your cousin and sister,[5]
Fianna Bucher

(Jan. 3, 1905)

---

[5]   Amy is the daughter of Fianna's uncle Christian Bucher. "Sister" means sister in Christ, not birth sister. This was common usage within Fianna's church community.

Father George continued to pour his energy into the church, traveling to preach at other congregations, as well as building up the congregation he had started. Fianna herself had been one of the first to become a member in the new congregation. She was baptized when she was 10 years old. In the Brethren tradition, baptism by immersion upon accepting Jesus as Savior brought one into church membership. It was an individual decision, not a decision made by one's parents.

Although it wasn't unusual to join the church at Fianna's young age, I wonder if her father influenced her decision. He wanted the congregation he had founded to succeed. The whole family was active in the church and invested in having it thrive. Her brother Rufus followed his father into the ministry. He was called to the ministry when he was 17 years old, and he continued to serve his home congregation for the rest of his life.

Fianna took on church work that was open to women. When she was 17, she was secretary for the Sunday School. In my attic, I found the Sunday School record book, and I was amazed by the details she recorded each week. She noted who had provided leadership—who led the prayer, who read which Bible passage, and who taught the lesson. She carefully listed the amount of offering collected (usually less than a dollar) and the weather of the day. When someone moved or died, that was recorded, too. Near the back of the book, she noted the treasurer's resignation and how the secretary (Fianna herself) took on that function.

Church involvement was central for the Bucher family,

but it was not without its challenges. There was friction within the congregation and, in fact, within the whole denomination. This was a time of change among the Brethren, and Fianna's father leaned toward the old ways. When Fianna was 20 years old, her parents left the German Baptist Brethren and joined the conservative branch of the denomination, the Old Order German Baptist Brethren. I wish I could have heard the conversations in their home during that time. George Bucher's energy had started this congregation 10 years earlier. He surely

Sunday School record keeping when Fianna was secretary

must have struggled, but he believed the church was moving in the wrong direction, and so he withdrew his membership.[6]

I wonder where Fianna worshipped for the next few years while she still lived at home. Her brother Rufus continued to minister to the congregation his father started. Perhaps she went to church with him.

A major exception to George Bucher's conservatism continued to be education. Not having had opportunity for formal education beyond eighth grade due to the church's attitude toward education in *his* childhood, he was determined to send all his children to college. He helped to start a church-supported school, Elizabethtown College, only 35 miles away, and he served as a trustee of the college. Son Rufus was in the first class of the new school in 1900, and Fianna followed a few years later.

---

[6]   *History of the Church of the Brethren of the Eastern District of Pennsylvania.* S. R. Zug, Chairman of the Committee, New Era Printing Co., 1915, p. 346-348.

CHAPTER 4

AWAY AT COLLEGE

Fianna's schooling between eighth grade at Prospect
School and her year at Elizabethtown College is unknown. She might have attended high school in the nearby
town of Quarryville, but it is more likely her public school
education ended with eighth grade. I think she stayed home
to help her mother since she was the only girl still there. Her
home environment definitely supported education, both
self-education and schooling. Fortunately for Fianna, in Elizabethtown College's early years, students did not need a high
school education to take classes. Fianna could still attend college, even if she ended her public schooling
with eighth grade.

In 1907, Fianna was 21 years old
and a new college student. According
to a crumbling, yellowed bill from
the College dated May 28, 1908,
her tuition for a 12-week term was
$12.00, while room and board were
$6.00 and $33.00 respectively. To off-
set this staggering amount, she received
a "minister's family" discount of $4.80.

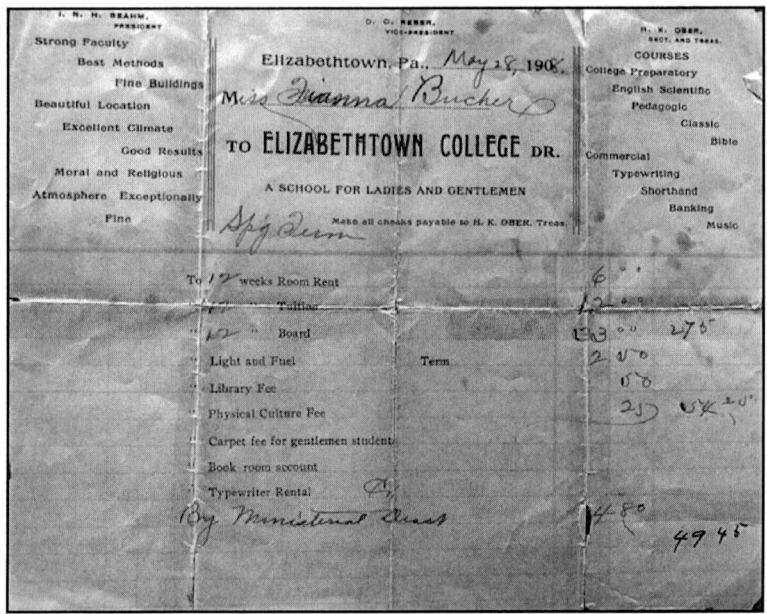

Elizabethtown College tuition bill

In Fianna's letters home, she recalled studying, going for walks, and being with other "girls" in her room. She wrote that she had dinner with "the Beahms." Her oldest sister Mary, who had left home and married when Fianna was four years old, now lived in Elizabethtown where her husband I. N. H. Beahm was President of the College.[7] How lovely to be a young adult and get re-acquainted with her big sister! Perhaps dinner with the Beahms allayed the homesickness that is evident in some of the letters she sent to her family. Although the letters below were addressed to sister Mary Phillipy (married to Phares Habecker), they were shared with Fianna's parents, and with her brother Rufus' family:

---

[7]   I. N. H. Beahm had been a professor at Bridgewater College in Virginia when Fianna's sister Mary was a student there.

My dear Sister:-

This is Sunday evening 9 o'clock P.M. - Post Meridian. I am one day nearer home . . . We are right in the midst of examinations. I don't bother my head very seriously about them. But I would like to get to bed a little early this evening as I want to get up early in the morning.

I expect to come home on Wed. evening. I am glad.

Lovingly, Your Sister

Fianna

(Nov. 24, 1907)

My Dear Sister:-

Your letter came today and I was very, very glad for it. I should have written sooner but I was real busy . . .

Wed. Morning. This is a very cold morning. I just took a walk and my hands are almost too cold to write . . .

Rufus, I think Physiology is the hardest branch I have. There are about thirty in the class. I don't get quite what I should like to.

I will enclose my report. We are expected to send them to our parents. Keep it till I come. I am afraid my marks won't be as good this term. I mean to try though . . .

Fianna

(Dec. 11, 1907)

After being home for Christmas, Fianna seemed to enjoy college more. Both the studies and the people interested her, and there were no more hints of homesickness. Perhaps January's Bible term brought more interesting learning for her. Fianna wrote her mother that "many people asked about you and father during B.T."[8]

She wrote about young men who showed attention to her:

My Dear Sister & all:-

This Sunday evening . . . we had a fine sermon on "Bible Study" by Bro. Falkenstein. This was the beginning of the Bible Term. I thought and talked about you today. The Bible students are beginning to file in . . .

On Monday morning when I came in the station at the Grove [for the trolley], John Greenleaf and Guy Winters were there. I did not know Mr. Winters till John told me. He said he knew me right away. He sat with me all the way to Lanc. In Lanc. he took the Columbia car. He said I could take the same car. So I did. He helped me off with my things there. He was very nice.

I would have lots to talk but hardly know what to write so I would better close. It is soon bed time. Prof. Meyer is coming tomorrow.

Lovingly,

Fianna

(Jan. 5, 1908)

I think "Prof. Meyer" was Samuel Meyer, her future husband. He also was a student at Elizabethtown College at this time, and he and his brothers sometimes called each other "professor." Was "Mr. Winters" competition for Samuel?

---

[8]   January "Bible Term" (B.T.) provided two weeks of intense Bible and religious study. College enrollment more than doubled during that time.

In a letter to her mother, she wrote about her youngest brother, twenty-year-old Willie, who still lived at home. He thought he wasn't ready for college. Fianna disagreed; she wanted to share this college experience with him:

I wish I could talk with Willie. I wish he were here in school. There are some here who are further back than he is. Oh! I almost get hot sometimes when I see how much I would like to learn till spring yet. I would like to see Willie's books and things. I am afraid he might overdo himself . . .

 Lovingly,

  Fianna

        (Jan. 20, 1908)

I remember visiting Uncle William Bucher with my parents when I was a child. He and his wife lived in the family farmhouse in rooms filled with books. In a news article about him when he was 81, he described himself as "self-educated."[9] He was a farmer and a local historian of some repute who had co-authored several church history books. Willie may not have followed his older siblings into college, but he certainly followed them into learning.

Although Fianna thought she should be learning more, by the time the spring term came around, she was doing so well that she was asked to teach when one of her instructors became ill:

My Dear Sister,

 Is it possible that this is the first of March? I can hardly real-

---

[9] *Lancaster Intelligencer,* August 31, 1970, p. 30.

ize that I have been away from home for five months now. About three months and a half now yet. In one way I am glad. In another I dread it. I shall be glad to be with the home folks again but it will be hard to part with all the dear girls, I think.

How are you all? . . . There has been so much sickness around here. . . I have a real bad cold again but am getting better. We are busy too. I taught Miss Foglesanger's U.S. History class all week and the way it looks now I will have it all [next] week. I think I must take U.S. History over next term. I am not getting near out of it what I ought to. It is real hard and of course we take long lessons . . .

I don't know much to write and there are three girls in my room and they want to talk.

Write soon.

Lovingly,

Fianna

(March 1, 1908)

Fianna held very high standards for herself.

Friendship was also an important aspect of the college experience. One of Fianna's close friends at college was Martha Martin. A few years later Martha was the Bible teacher at the College, a position she held long enough to be Bible teacher for Fianna's children when they, in their turn, became Elizabethtown College students.[10]

It was a close-knit Brethren world for these young

---

[10]   Martha Martin was also a friend to my maternal grandmother, Annis Wenger, and a teacher for both my parents when they were Elizabethtown College students.

women and men. Church meetings, marriages within the denomination, and large families created a strong web of relationships. Postcards between Fianna and Martha describe a treasured friendship well before their college days. Fianna sent this postcard to Martha the year before she attended Elizabethtown:

My Dear Sister:-

Your letter reached me some time ago and was highly appreciated. "Many many thanks" for that beautiful book mark you sent me. Accept my love in return . . .

Your sister,

Fianna P. Bucher

(Sept. 12, 1906)

CHAPTER 5

A College Romance

For me, Fianna's most interesting friendship is the one with her future husband. Although Samuel Meyer and Fianna were students together, they had probably known each other much earlier. They lived over fifty miles apart, but both families were very active in the life of the denomination. Their grandfathers were first cousins, and they would have attended the same family reunions. Samuel's father, like Fianna's father, was a strong supporter of Elizabethtown College and encouraged his children to attend.

So Fianna and Samuel were acquainted with each other before they ate regularly in the same dining room, before they saw each other at chapel services and took the same classes. I imagine theirs to be a college romance. Fianna was 22 and Samuel was 23, and I think they began to see each other with new eyes that year.

According to the college newspaper, *Our College Times,* both Fianna and Samuel were active in the

"Keystone Literary Society." Samuel served as president of the Society that year. An article in *Our College Times* informed the reader that Miss F. Bucher had read an "Essay on Lincoln" for the February 1908 meeting of the Society.[11] I can picture Fianna standing before the members reading her essay with Samuel sitting nearby, listening intently and full of appreciation for her work.

After her year at college, Fianna returned home to live with her parents and Willie. In reading *Our College Times*, I discovered that she passed the "creditable" examination to receive a teachers' certificate for the "beginners classes."[12]

Samuel also left the college and returned home. He taught school the next year to earn money so he could return to study one more year. This was very common during that time. *Our College Times* informed me that Samuel received two diplomas from the College: an English Scientific diploma in 1908 and a Pedagogical diploma in 1910.[13]

I wonder how much Samuel and Fianna were able to see each other during the next two years before they married. One postcard to her friend Clara mentions Fianna's visit to her and how they had visited Samuel's home in Fredericksburg:

---

[11] *Our College Times,* March 1908, p. 9.

[12] Although Fianna was accredited, I have no information that she actually taught.

[13] Elizabethtown College was not an accredited degree institution during its early years; students received diplomas instead. Graduation ceremonies were marked by orations from graduates. In 1908, Samuel spoke on "Four Cycles," and in 1910, on "Our Heritage." *Our College Times,* July 1908, p. 7, and *Our College Times,* July 1910, p. 11.

. . . You were all so kind to me that I can hardly be grateful enough. Just think of our ironing, taffy eating, writing letters and especially that memorable trip to Fredericksburg. Happy recollections! . . .

(Jan. 28, 1909)

I have four mysterious postcards that I think Samuel sent to Fianna. Two are particularly mysterious. One has only a large question mark for a message. The other one is a Valentine's Day card, sent in 1908 when Fianna and Samuel were students together. It simply contains the message: "U Know." I can imagine Fianna's happy smile when she received it! While she may have had other admirers sending cards, I think she kept these unsigned cards because she knew they came from Samuel.

The other two cards are postmarked from Fredericksburg and are signed "Hiawatha." Hiawatha was Samuel's special name just between the two of them. Longfellow's *Song of Hiawatha* was very popular during the early 1900s. Perhaps Samuel and Fianna had taken a literature class together and discovered it. Perhaps they fell in love with Longfellow through the meetings of the Keystone Literary Society while falling in love with each other. Tucked in the box with Fianna's letters, I found two small booklets of selections and illustrations from Longfellow's *Evangeline*. I picture Samuel and Fianna reading *Evangeline* and *Hiawatha* and other popular Longfellow poems to each other during that precious college year.

I knew my grandfather Samuel wrote poetry, and I have

Hiawatha postcard from Samuel to Fianna

copies of some that he wrote later in his life. But I never realized that meant he must have *loved* poetry, too. How delightful to discover that my grandparents' romance included sharing this love!

The first "Hiawatha" postcard suggests Samuel hoped to visit Fianna's home on his way back to school:

> *On account of book room [library] I ought to be at college early Monday. I thought of going via Etown Saturday, leave my substance there and come down P.M. Do I have your consent to this?*
>
> *Hiawatha*
>
> (1909)

Springtime turned Samuel's thoughts to his sweetheart as he worked at home one weekend:

*Am planting corn, beans, etc. The ground is in the best
condition. May return tomorrow on the wheel. Wish I could send
you some lilacs. They are most fragrant.*
        Hiawatha

           (May 7, 1910)

One month later Samuel graduated from Elizabethtown
College. A few weeks after that Fianna and Samuel were married. This printed announcement was sent out to friends and
relatives.

In their wedding picture, the young couple is very serious.
As was the custom, the groom was seated and Fianna stood by
his side, her slenderness emphasized by her plain white dress. A
marrying dress at this time was not a special wedding dress but
a good dress to be worn again in the future. Every time I look at
the picture of my hopeful young grandparents, I think of their
five short years together. And I know this is the dress she will
be buried in.

Miss Fianna P. Bucher

and

Mr. Samuel G. Meyer

announce their marriage

Tuesday, June the twenty-eighth

nineteen hundred and ten

at the home of the bride

Quarryville, Penna.

At Home

after July twelfth

Fredericksburg, Penna.

Wedding picture and announcement

CHAPTER 6

EARLY MARRIED LIFE

I have no letters from the first year of Fianna and Samuel's life together. They may have lived on the family farm with Samuel's parents. It was not unusual for young couples to do that. By August of the following year, however, when their first child, Ammon, was born, they had their own home. Living just over a hill from Samuel's parents' farm, they were close enough to receive help if they needed it, and to give help, too. But Samuel was not primarily a farmer. He supported his young family by working as the cashier in the Fredericksburg bank that his father had helped to create.

For the first time in her life, Fianna lived at a distance from her family, that vibrant nest of Buchers who had spread out to include several farms and families. She had joined the Meyer clan, another large, vibrant Brethren family. It wasn't so far from their home near Fredericksburg to the Bucher farm south of Quarryville—only 60 miles—but it was far for Fianna. A visit was a rare and much anticipated event. One always planned to stay for a while, perhaps for several weeks.

After returning from a visit to her parents with her six-month-old baby, Fianna wrote a letter to her mother filled with stories of their trip home and details of daily life:

Dear Mother:-

No doubt you are anxious to hear how we got home so I thought I would write a letter. We got along fine. In Lancaster a lady that I did not know put the suitcase on the car for me. Then there was a River sister on the Manheim car[14] . . . She carried Ammon up to the station for me. She went up there especially to help me. Then there was a young girl at the station that carried the suitcase on the train for me. In Lebanon [hired man] John was at the station. Ammon was very good. He slept and kicked and crowed. I guess he got tired . . .

I feel a little lonely but I will soon forget it when I get to work. I am very tired too.

Our chickens are doing fine. We found 2 doz. yesterday. It is something new to see our egg basket filling up.

I am sitting on your cushion to write this. It is nice and soft. The dried beef was so good. There is a little here yet I can eat for dinner. Samuel put the nest eggs out this morning.

I want to wash Ammon's things today and sew what time I have left.

Samuel is pleased to take the incubator and brooder at that price but we cannot pay it before April. I am anxious to have it to attend to. It will be so nice to have little chickens.

I must stop and dress Ammon.

Lovingly,

Fianna

(Feb. 20, 1912)

---

[14] "River sister" refers to another Anabaptist sect known as the River Brethren.

A trip like Fianna's, between the Bucher parents' home and the Meyer home, was a major undertaking. It included at least three trolley or train rides, as well as waiting at the stations in between. And buggy rides were needed for travel to the stations on either end. Fianna's train from Quarryville, the small town closest to her parents' farm, took her to Lancaster

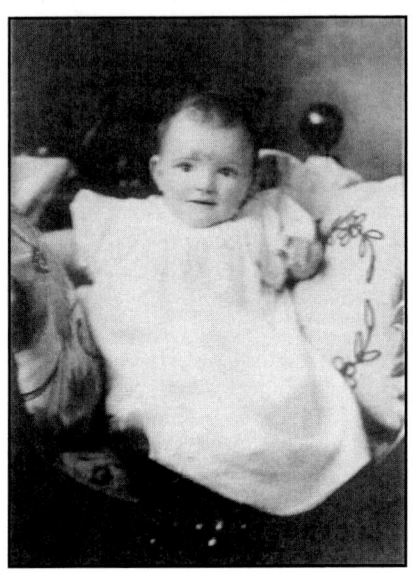

Ammon Bucher Meyer

in approximately an hour. In the larger, bustling Lancaster station, she switched to "the Manheim car" which would carry her to the village of Manheim, where she would wait for the train to Lebanon. How exhausting it must have been, especially with a baby in her arms. I am glad fellow travelers helped this young mother.

When I was a child, my grandfather Samuel raised chickens, and I remember watching hundreds of them clucking within a large enclosed yard at his farm. The letter above recounts his start as a chicken farmer. Working with chickens was familiar work for Fianna. She was eager to begin caring for chicks in the incubator that she and Samuel wanted to buy from her parents. She also wrote about "nest eggs." These were artificial eggs placed in a nest to encourage a hen to lay eggs there and sit on them until they hatched.

Homemaking and parenting in the early 1900s was exhausting work. Before her marriage, Fianna's life had included several Bucher women joining together for the work, particularly food preservation and sewing projects. She and her mother, her sister Mary, and her brother Rufus' wife Naomi all lived close to each other. It's understandable that she felt "a little lonely" after a visit with her family. She missed the working companionship of her mother and sisters, but I think she also missed their delight in her sweet little boy.

Although they lived too far apart for easy visiting, Fianna's mother still yearned to help her youngest daughter. Fianna replied reassuringly to her mother's concern:

Dear Mother and all:-

I have put dinner on the stove and while that is getting ready I want to write a few lines . . .

If you have any crabapples to make jelly make it for yourself. We have some too yet and we don't eat much. You have enough work without that. And don't worry about filling those cans either. We have fruit perhaps more than you do. We have apples and lots of pears later on. I canned 16 qts. of peaches last week.

Yesterday we were at Zeiglers' church and children's meeting. Today is our council at Merkey's about nine miles from here.[15] *We did not go. I didn't feel so well and Samuel doesn't like to leave his work too often . . .*

---

[15] "Merkeys" and "Zieglers" were names of two small church buildings where congregational worship services were held.

I must look after my dinner and Ammon. He is keeping house in the kitchen. I don't know what he is doing but I hear a bumping once in a while . . .

We expect to have some apple butter boiled this week. I am hungry for it long already.

Love to all,

Fianna

(undated, probably 1912)

Church and family, family and church: these shaped Fianna and Samuel's life together. Fianna wrote a long letter to sister Mary telling her about a whole weekend of services focusing on Sunday School work that was hosted by their local church. Everyone assisted in the effort to find beds and meals for participants from other congregations who came from a distance. Samuel and Fianna invited visitors into their house. They were even willing to sleep—or try to sleep—on the floor:

My dear Sister:-

This is Sunday evening and a cold one at that. It certainly feels good to be by the stove. Samuel is sitting here sleeping and I already feel my eyes are getting heavy . . .

Well, we had our S.S. meeting at the Union House yesterday. It was interesting and fairly well attended. [Six persons] were here for supper . . . After the meeting an automobile full of people came along home with us for the night . . . We had the beds filled with strangers. We slept on the floor and [hired man] Jesse on the couch. I just slept a few hours. Our bed wasn't very good, it was late when we got there and then I was thinking too much. I didn't sleep much before one and not after half past three. Do you wonder I am tired? But we enjoyed their visit ever so much. This morning we had to hurry to get to church in time in Fredericksburg.

We were at Grandparents for dinner. They had 30 some to dinner and had roast duck. This afternoon we were in S.S. again. It feels good to be at home this evening . . .

I wish mother could hear all the compliments I have received about Ammon's coat. Lots have asked me whether I made it and I am proud to say mother did it. He also wore the new cap Naomi made yesterday and today. He looks cute. At first he didn't trust to turn his head with his new cap on. He would just turn his eyes.

Last Thursday afternoon we were in Leb. and spent a lot of money not unnecessary though. I have a stack of sewing to do now. We got a second hand coal stove for $8.00. We want to keep warm this winter. Also got a dear little buggy . . . Samuel said we should write your name on every spoke of the wheels. I wish you could see it . . . we tell people it is a gift from you . . . Ammon likes it. We put him in there while we did our shopping . . . Samuel and Jesse took him along in a clothing store. There they gave him his bottle and went about their business. After a while they looked and he was standing on the seat looking back over the buggy top . . .

With much love,

Fianna

(Nov. 3, 1912)

In a letter to her mother, Fianna depicted an ordinary evening at home for the family. Samuel's work in the bank carried over into the evening. I can picture Samuel with "his books" at one end of a wooden kitchen table, and Fianna with her writing tablet sitting at the other end, both of them sleepy after a long day of work:

Dear Mother and all:-

While Samuel is fixing his books I will write a few lines for home. He said he is glad I want to write too so I will get my thoughts collected. He gets bothered if I talk too much but the fact is I like to talk when I have some one to talk to. I have been alone so much this week . . .

I wish I could see those little dresses you want to surprise Ammon with.[16] I can hardly wait. I made two for every day but it will come in handy to have more. Especially if he keeps on getting into mischief then he will dirty them . . .

Love to all,

   Fianna

(undated)

Even if many miles separated the Bucher family from Fianna, they helped the young couple as much as they could. Mother offered to make jelly or preserve fruit. She sent food home with them after a visit. Naomi made Ammon's cap, and Mother made a coat and several dresses for the toddler. Sister Mary and her husband sent money so they could buy

---

[16]   Little boys like Ammon wore dresses, often until they were three or four years old.

a baby buggy for Ammon. The Bucher women continued to look out for the youngest daughter among them as she created her home.

CHAPTER 7

A SECOND CHILD—LEAH

The second baby in this growing family was named Leah (for Fianna's sister as well as Samuel's mother) and arrived on a cold day in January 1913. I wonder how long it took for the news of the new birth to travel to the Bucher families sixty miles away. Fianna's sister Mary Habecker cared for little Ammon while Fianna recovered from childbirth, and Fianna clearly missed him. One Sunday evening she wrote wistfully to her sister Mary, wondering about Ammon and describing daily life with the new little one:

Dear Sister & all:-

It is just about 6 o'clock p.m. It is just "between the dark and the twilight, As the day is beginning to lower." I am all alone and to drive away a sort of lonesomeness I thought I would write you a letter.

Samuel & Jesse have gone to Freystown to church & S.S. . . . Leah is sleeping. . . . I guess I will go to bed early. The evening won't seem so long if I sleep . . .

We are getting along very well. We have a very good baby. She sleeps nearly all the time. She is growing and getting fat. I

begin to feel well now and shall be glad to see my little boy soon
again . . . Where did you have Ammon when you taught your
class these Sundays? I am glad you have him down there . . . and
I am glad he is so contented and happy.

It is getting windy and cloudy this evening, too. It may not
be a very good wash day tomorrow . . . I am glad I have somebody
good to do the washing.

We weighed the baby today. She weighs 9 lbs. now. As much
as Ammon did when he was born . . .

Lovingly

Fianna

P.S. I am always so glad to hear. I usually read your mail over
and over again.

(Feb. 9, 1913)

The quotation at the beginning of this letter is from the poem
"The Children's Hour" recounting a father's love for his children. Like the *Song of Hiawatha,* it was written by Longfellow. I can picture Samuel and Fianna reading "The Children's
Hour" together and thinking of their own children.

Fianna wrote that she had a "sort of lonesomeness." She
wished she were closer to her family, and, even though she read
their letters "over and over," it wasn't enough. She wanted to
share the new baby. That Ammon was with them was a joy, but
what she wanted most was to talk with sister Mary or with her
mother. Like the day, her mood was lowered.

Fianna was most likely tired, too. Babies were even more
work a century ago than they are now. There were no auto-

matic washing machines or disposable diapers for babies. There were no easy, no-iron fabrics. There were definitely no dryers to simplify things. In wintertime, wet laundry was hung above the stove, in the basement, or outdoors to freeze-dry. I was glad to discover that Fianna had help during this time, at least someone to help with laundry.

Although she received regular cards or letters from family, especially from her Phillipy sisters Mary and Leah, it was unusual to receive a letter from brother Rufus. He was a busy farmer and minister and much in demand as an evangelist. I only wish he could spell better! I don't think she cared about his spelling; she was simply glad to receive his note:

Dear Sister,

Except my congratulations for the one who has come to increase the Bucher and Myer relationship. May she grow to be useful in the Master's service.

Hopeing you are all well. I am at Middle Creek. I am working hard. Good meetings, good interest, four converts, others near.

Yours as ever,

Rufus P. Bucher

(Jan. 24, 1913)

A few months later Fianna wrote more cheerfully. Her health restored, she was working harder than ever. In the second letter below, she wished for the same thing many young mothers wish for, a grandmother available for baby-sitting. There was no end to the tasks that needed her attention, and having a baby and a toddler definitely slowed her down.

Letter writing was an evening activity. After the hard physical work of the day was over, Fianna used the quiet evening time to take out her writing paper and share the events of daily life with her Bucher family:

Dear Mother & all:-

This is Monday evening and I am alone with my little brood. Samuel does not expect to be here before nine or ten o'clock . . . The baby is awake in the coach and is watching the light. I guess she will soon want to go to sleep for the night. She is very good and laughs a lot and I am glad too. Since [hired man] Jesse left, I milk and feed and do more outdoor work than I used to. I enjoy it too. I usually fix Ammon some way so he can't get at the baby when I go out like that.

Oh I mustn't forget to tell you we are weaning Ammon from his bottle. He sleeps so well at night so I thought this would be a good time . . . He is getting along fine. The first time I put him to bed without it he didn't cry at all. On Sat. evening he woke up and hunted under his covers and all around for it. He had to cry a little sometimes but it didn't last long. This evening I put his rag baby to bed with him and he didn't cry a bit when I went down . . . He gets so hungry now. As soon as he is down in the morning he begs for something to eat . . .

Much love,

Fianna

(April 7, 1913)

Fianna and her family tried to write each week. I can imagine how eagerly she looked for the rural mail carrier's daily delivery. Would there be a letter from home for her?

Dear Mother:-

It is late and is bedtime but if I can keep my eyes open long enough I want to write a few lines home yet. If I don't send it tomorrow you won't get it this week any more. Samuel is sitting here sleeping and Ammon is sitting on his high chair looking at the pictures and talks about them. He talks a good bit more than he did when we were home . . . Leah had a bad cold but seems to be getting all right again . . .

I was looking for a letter from home all week. There are two more days. I did not give it up for this week yet.

I made two night gowns and a dress for Ammon, a night shirt for Samuel, did up the mending I had lying around and washed and ironed this week . . . I wish we could be together with our sewing some times. I still have some on hand. We may go to Lebanon on Sat. afternoon. Then I will get more. I wish you were here to care for the children . . .

Write soon. I am anxious to hear.

Fianna

(undated, probably 1913)

By winter, Fianna was pregnant again and due to give birth in February. I wonder how strong she was, whether she was still doing the outdoor work or whether Fianna and Samuel hired someone to help with the farm work.

The exchange of letters continued to be very important for

Fianna and her family, but something new had entered the picture by this time. The telephone had arrived in rural Pennsylvania! It had even come into Fianna's farmhouse! When there was important news to be given, one simply called the "exchange" and asked for a connection. But sometimes the connection wasn't so clear, and those on the other end couldn't understand the speaker:

Dear Homefolks[17]*:-*

It does not seem as though I were so far from home when we can just take down the receivers and talk together. I was sorry you could not understand me so well on Sat. morning. I could hear you well.

Rufus called up from Annville this morning. I could hardly hear him but he said father is getting along well. We are glad to hear that. We were glad for father's letter. We decided it ought to be read like the Chinese read, that is begin at the hind end.

... Grandfather Gibbels[18] *are butchering this week. Grandmother sent word that I should send her some buttermilk on Friday and then she would give us a sausage. She knows I am hungry for some. I suppose they want to bake cakes for X'mas with the buttermilk ...*

We were in Lebanon on Sat. afternoon. Oh! but it was crowded. I hope I will never need to go so near Christmas time again. It seems

---

[17]   Many of Fianna and Samuel's letters were addressed to "Homefolks," and sent to Fianna's parents. These letters were shared among the Bucher families living close by.

[18]   Samuel's grandparents' (Joseph and Elizabeth) last name is spelled *Gibbel* on their tombstones. The tombstone of their daughter, Samuel's mother, reads Leah *Gibble* Meyer. I have used the spelling for each person as engraved on the tombstone.

the people are crazy. We got carpet for the stairway and a good soft mattress for our bed. I wish you could sleep on it . . .

I am so anxious to see you and talk with you all. It would be a great disappointment if you wouldn't come. Get father to write again. I said to Samuel, "I guess father does lots of writing just now."

Lovingly,

Fianna

(Dec. 15, 1913)

Although early telephone conversations were sometimes difficult, written communications also presented challenges. I wish I had a copy of father George's letter that "ought to be read like the Chinese read." A letter from him was a rarity, but while he was recovering from his illness, he had time to write. Even if the letters were hard to read, the recipients were very glad to receive them.

Written ten days before Christmas, Fianna's letter above described her hopes that her parents would come to her house for a Christmas visit. She was probably considering what food she'd have for dinner or whom they would visit. She was eager to share her daily life with her mother. She would be especially eager to show her parents how much her children had grown since they last saw them. She even had a new mattress she hoped her parents would sleep on.

Fianna wasn't sure her parents would visit, and, in fact, they didn't come until January. However, someone brought Samuel and Fianna cakes that her mother and sister Mary had made for the Christmas festivities:

Dear Parents & all,

. . . Tell Mary we enjoyed her cake ever so much. She must have gone to a lot of trouble. We have a little yet and some of yours too. I just baked one cake and we have about half of that yet. They don't go so fast here.

Tomorrow is wash day and the engine is only nine miles away. A good bit nearer than last Monday. Maybe by next Monday it will be here . . .

With much love,

Fianna

P.S. Samuel wants to get someone to bring the engine tomorrow or we must pay storage. I guess I wrote enough about it that you know I appreciate it.

(Dec. 28, 1913)

This "engine" is a washing machine. How did she wash clothes before she had it? Was there another, more primitive "engine" or did she use something like a scrubbing board? This machine was a gift from her parents and had been helped along its way to her, hitching rides with Brethren friends who were traveling her direction. "Nine miles away"—so near and yet so far.

In early January, her parents finally came for a visit. Fianna wrote to them, "I have fresh sausage and a pork roast on hand for you." What joy she must have had to finally have her parents at her table!

CHAPTER 8

THE HARD TIMES—BABY RUFUS

Samuel sent news of the birth of baby Rufus (named for Fianna's brother) to Fianna's parents:

Dear Parents:-
"I arrived here Feb. 11th. I came on a very cold day at 9:30 P.M. My name is—Rufus Bucher Meyer."
P.S. Fianna is well. Better than any time before . . . Ammon is with [Samuel's brother] Levi's.
                    Samuel
                                        (Feb. 13, 1914)

But six weeks later Fianna had to send her parents a very different message:

Dear Homefolks:-
We have a very sick baby. Dr. Wise from Leb. and Dr. Kerr held a consultation here this forenoon. Dr. Wise says it is milk infection. Its lungs are all right. The trouble is in the stomach & bowels. We dare not feed any milk for the present. . . . I hope it may still come all right but it is so very weak. We look to a higher power.
                    Fianna
                                        (April 29, 1914)

Baby Rufus died the same day Fianna sent this message to her parents. Grieving together, Fianna and Samuel's families gathered for the funeral. Fianna's parents had never met this little grandson before they lost him.

Afterwards, when everyone had left, and Fianna and Samuel were alone with their pain, came the hardest time. Although sister Mary cared for their little Leah, Ammon stayed with his parents. He was just two years old, and he didn't understand what had happened:

Dear Sister:-

I suppose you wish to know how we are. [Brother] Rufus took Sam'l and me to the Dr. . . . The Dr. thinks I am much better. He said one lung is almost clear and the other is a little sore yet. He said it was pleurisy . . . He talked very consoling about the baby. He told me not to brood. I do try. Last evening after everybody was gone I tried to be brave. Then Ammon came and said, "I can't find baby Rufus." I tried to explain. Then after a little he went upstairs. I thought of nothing. Then he came down and said, "I can't find baby Rufus. Mamma, find baby Rufus." That was too much for me. Write soon.

F.

(May 4, 1914)

Fianna could not find "baby Rufus" for his big brother Ammon. And Ammon was still too young to understand about dying—or why his mother cried. Fianna's sister Leah replied to Fianna as soon as she could:

My dear sister,

I have a little time this afternoon so I thought I would take it and write to you. It is the only way that I can let you know that I am thinking of you in your sorrow. I am glad you can be so brave. I think Ammon's searching for baby is so pathetic. I don't wonder that it was too much for you. I hope he will soon forget it as he can not understand and it makes it so hard for you. I wish I could spend some of my spare moments with you and do all for you I can. But I am glad you have Lizzie [house helper] and that she is so good and kind.

I am glad you are getting better, take good care of yourself, go out all you can, dress up and sit out on the porch in the fresh air, it is the best thing you can do, but wrap up good . . .

I would like to see you all.

Your loving sister

Leah

P.S. I don't ask a letter from you but send a card sometimes so I know how you are. I am anxious about you.

(May 6, 1914)

In the card to sister Leah, Fianna had written, "everybody was gone." I imagine her alone in the house with Ammon. Perhaps it was late afternoon, and Samuel had taken someone to the train station or returned to the bank to catch up with his work. Her parents were on their way back home. Brother Rufus and his family, sister Mary and her family, brother William were all returning to their own lives.

Sister Leah had returned to Lancaster and her work as a housekeeper, but she wrote often. In one letter to Fianna, she wrote about the funeral. She wanted Fianna to know how the baby's death had touched her. She also told her how their nephew Caleb, a six year old, and his younger sister Martha were affected by their baby cousin's death:

My dear sister:-

. . . to write a few lines to you to let you know I am thinking of you. I suppose mother will soon be leaving now. I wish I could be with you now for a few days. I am so glad that you are both so reconciled in your sorrow and feel that it was the Lord's will that baby should only be with you for such a short time . . .

. . . I don't know if anybody told you that Caleb had to cry so the first evening when they found out about the baby dying. Naomi said he cried because God took the baby. When we walked in to the church from the grave I had Martha on one side and Caleb on the other side of me. Martha talked about it but Caleb looked like he was thinking seriously and never said a word. Rufus looked back and said, "I would like to read that mind." He soon fell asleep in the church and I was glad that he did not hear Bro. Wenger[19] preach. Martha asked sometimes during the sermon about the baby if it is buried now . . .

On Thursday while at dinner I look out and everything was so beautiful especially the cherry tree in our yard which is so full of blossoms. I thought how beautiful and I thought of your baby now blooming in a fairer world than this. I liked Bro. Wenger as he expressed himself that baby Rufus was only plucked from the

---

[19]   Bro. Edward M. Wenger was the presiding minister of the congregation and Samuel's uncle.

garden below and was transplanted in the garden above where he is now blooming to perfection.

When I looked on that lifeless little form I thought I don't know that I ever saw anything more beautiful than this. So pure, just as God gave it he took it.

May God richly bless you both and I pray that you may soon recover and bring up your two little jewels to be used in His service.

With much love,
Leah

(May 3, 1914)

CHAPTER 9

THE HARD TIMES—
FIANNA'S DECLINE

Although Samuel had written that Fianna was "better than any time before" when he announced Rufus' birth, she didn't regain her health in the following months. Their doctor called it "pleurisy." This condition is an inflammation of membranes surrounding the lungs and it causes pain and breathlessness. I have no letters Fianna wrote during the winter or spring of 1914. Perhaps she had no energy to write and used the telephone when she needed to communicate. I wonder what she did in the evening when she and Samuel were together in the kitchen, the time when she used to write letters. Was she so tired that she fell asleep in her chair as Samuel occasionally did in his?

Grief also sapped her energy, making it even harder to recover. And, although she didn't know it, she already had tuberculosis—the disease that would kill her less than a year later.

I have no letters written by Fianna during this time, but I have many letters written to her. Although she had six older half-sisters, four of them had married and moved far away. Inevitably those relationships were less close. Only Mary, married to Phares Habecker and living close to the Bucher homestead in southern Lancaster County, and Leah, living and working in the city of Lancaster, remained intimate. Receiving their letters, knowing how deeply they loved her, gave Fianna much needed support and encouragement.

Sister Leah's letters expressed her love and anxiety. Older than Fianna by twelve years, she had helped raise her little sister. Leah never married, and her birth family remained central in her life. But she had her job and couldn't leave and care for her sister whenever she wanted to. Even before the baby died, Leah had written:

My dear sister:-

I was very glad for your letter yesterday . . . I do not think that you complained at all. I am glad you gave me the facts and I want nothing but the truth when you do write no matter what it is. I want to give you good advice now, do by all means as the doctor tells you to and if your work don't go on as usual. Don't clean house and if you do get better and feel able to do it use your strength for something else and when my vacation comes I'll come and clean it for you and if I don't get a vacation I'll come and do it any how. Samuel and I can shake the carpet and see who is the stronger. It will just be a little later that is all.

With much love,

Leah

(April 17, 1914)

During this hard time, Fianna's little Leah frequently stayed with sister Mary, but two-year-old Ammon remained at home. Fianna wasn't strong enough to care for both children. Once sister Leah wrote about playing with her namesake on a visit to Mary, and then she added, "I am glad you are making the sacrifice." Leah understood how hard it was for Fianna to give her daughter into another's care.

Mary and her husband Phares were happy to care for one-year-old Leah. The little girl spent some of the summer with her parents, but when Fianna became more seriously ill in the autumn, Leah was returned to live with Mary and Phares. She lived with them until she was four years old. Even after she moved back to be with her father and brother, her life included long summer visits to her Aunt Mary. Mary and Phares provided her with a home where she was treasured and deeply loved.

When Mary wrote to Fianna, she focused on daily life on the farm, church activities, and, of course, Leah. But she also wrote of her anxiety for her sister. In this letter, written just before baby Rufus died, Mary encouraged Fianna to consider a special service of healing that the church offered, the service of anointing:

Dear Sister and Family:-

I enjoyed the day [of church services] but I would have enjoyed it more yet if your little one and you would be blessed with health as we are. But take good care of yourselves. If you can help it, don't become discouraged, don't become blue, and don't worry about anything. If your house is not as you would like to have it, if your garden don't get tended to, if the fence don't get whitewashed, if the children are not as tidy as you would like them to be, don't let these things pull you down. If only I was closer I would gladly help you out some.

Many have been run down further yet then what you are and were restored to health again. And I hope and believe you will, too. Fianna did you ever give James 5 a thought? That is a command that is hardly ever kept until a person is sick almost unto death. Now the scripture does not say that way, it says, is any sick among you let him call for the elders, etc. What are you, are you sick or are you well? You didn't enjoy health for the last three months. Now I am not saying you shall do it. The scripture does not say that way. You are to call. I am just reminding you of it . . .

No you did not act queer when you were home. You acted wonderfully nice. But you were about nice people all the time, especially when you were with me . . .

Tomorrow is wash day. Am getting sleepy. Write before long and tell me all about the baby and yourself. Don't keep any thing from me. You and I always stuck together and we will yet. I will stick to you anyhow.

Mary

(April 20, 1914)

The ritual of anointing with oil followed a New Testament teaching. "Is any among you sick? Let them call the elders of the church to pray over them and anoint them in the name of the Lord."[20] It was more commonly requested when someone was near death, but, as Mary points out, the scripture doesn't limit anointing to that extremity. The Bible simply asks, "Is any among you sick?" I believe Mary's letter encouraged Fianna to ask the church elders for anointing.

---

[20] James 5:14.

An undated letter was given to Mary when Samuel delivered the little girl sometime after Rufus' death. In it, Fianna described a service in their home, most likely the anointing service:

Dear Mary:-

. . . We had a beautiful service last evening. Brethren Wenger and Pfautz[21] were here. I never felt nearer heaven in my life. I was stronger today but I am demanding too much of my strength. I am getting Leah's things ready. I am sending lots of clothes as she soon needs summer clothes . . .

We give our darling girl in your hands for an indefinite time. We will miss her as I have no other baby to hug now. But we think it is for the best. She is too strong for me and I know she will be well cared for. She has a little cold and is teething and is constipated too . . . I didn't want to send her in this busy time. But it does me a lot of good that you are glad for her. When I am stronger . . . I would like to come home for a week or so.

Whatever you do don't <u>keep Samuel</u>. . . .

Lovingly,

     Fianna

Write often if you have time.

(probably May or June 1914)

Mary followed Fianna's request to "write often," and she enlivened all her letters with stories about Fianna's little girl (often called "Dolly" by her family).

---

[21]   Bro. Edward M. Wenger and Bro. Jacob Pfautz were ministers in their congregation.

My dear Sister:-
    ... Had her along to the cow stable one evening, and one of the little calves we are raising stuck its long black tongue out and took a hold of her dress. I wished you could have seen her face and heard the objections she made ...

    Want to wash tomorrow. Also churn about 20 lbs of butter. Caleb, Martha, Dorothy, Beulah and Dolly had the german measles.[22] Dolly is just getting over them. They were not sick ...

                                                    Mary

                                        (May 25, 1914)

One of Mary's letters included a note from Fianna's mother: "Leah is a sweet little thing we are look forward till Satterday for your coming. Hope you are well." How hard it was to live so far away from her beloved youngest daughter, to know how much she needed help—and to be powerless to give help or bring her closer!

This note from Fianna's mother may have been especially treasured because she didn't write very much or easily in English. Fianna and Samuel and their families lived in a bilingual world. The older generation spoke Pennsylvania German among themselves, and Fianna's mother was more comfortable writing in Pennsylvania German than English. I know she sometimes wrote to her daughter in Pennsylvania German although I have no copies of her letters. Postcards to her grand-

---

[22] Caleb, Martha and Dorothy were little Leah's cousins. Beulah was a foster child living with Mary and her husband Phares.

children often had just "Granma" or "love, Granma" as the written message.

I loved reading about Samuel in this letter from Mary:

Dear Sister:

. . . I wonder how you are. Tell me. And your good man. Do you know what Kate Shenk said? You couldn't have gotten a better man if you would have traveled over the whole world.

Good night,

Mary

(undated)

I know he was a good, gentle, loving man because I knew him as a good, gentle, loving grandfather, but I was glad to read that others, knowing him as a young man, appreciated him, too. I can't imagine his pain as he watched Fianna continue to decline and as his little family was repeatedly separated.

I don't know how Samuel's family of Meyers and Gibbles/ Gibbels supported Fianna and him during this time. Since they lived close by, there was no need for written messages. Sometimes Fianna's letters describe sharing farm produce and preserved food with Samuel's family. I think there was a lot of daily interaction, but perhaps not the kind of on-going help Fianna needed.

The Bucher clan helped as much as they could. In July 1914, Samuel wrote to Fianna's parents and thanked them for the "letter that came to our mailbox some days ago with a hundred dollar check in it." Fianna's poor health created extra expenses with medical bills and household assistance. A century ago one hundred dollars was a *lot* of money!

In an unusual letter from Fianna's father George, he explained that he was writing as his wife's amanuensis—or scribe. Great-grandfather, you stumped me, even if it took a century. I had to look up *amanuensis* in a dictionary. But couldn't you spell *Meyer* correctly. I wonder if the address and signature were formal because of the contents of the letter or whether he always wrote with this formality. Fianna's father wanted Fianna and Samuel to know that the Buchers were downsizing:

S.G. & F.B. Meyrs,
Dear Children:-

Again I am my queen's amanuensis. In two weeks from last Saturday (April 4) Mam and I will leave Quarryville at 5:30 A.M. for Lebanon & Pinegrove . . .[23]

Mam thinks everything of her grand-daughter, Leah. I do not think she saw her since last Thursday a week when the Habeckers butchered . . .

We give Willie the farms and the stock. I wrote the various pieces of personal property in several books and gave them to Aaron, Rufus, Willie, and Allen respectively to price them . . . I made it $3000.00. I kept Kate, Dash the cows, the chickens, the little sleigh, the spring wagon, the carriage, and last but not least Grand-ma.

Respectfully & Fraternally,
Geo. & Fianna Bucher

(Mar. 23, 1914)

---

[23] Fianna's father traveled widely to preach. The small town of Pinegrove was not far from Samuel and Fianna's home. It appears that Fianna's parents planned to visit Samuel and Fianna on this trip.

These were important changes. Youngest son Willie would receive the homestead, as well as his father's second farm. They would keep horses Kate and Dash, who pulled the sleigh, the wagon, and the carriage. And, most important of all, Fianna's father decided to keep Grandma!

CHAPTER 10

BACK AND FORTH
THROUGH THE SUMMER

In June, Fianna and Ammon made the arduous, but much anticipated, trip to visit her family, and Fianna took little Leah with her when she returned home. While Fianna was away, Samuel wrote:

My dear Fianna, Ammon and Leah:-
I feel very much single these days . . . I was to Freystown to church. Brother Hollinger preached well on "The secret part of religion." I found my dinner at Br. Emanuel Balsbach's table . . .

Most of Samuel's letter is filled with church news but he does have some homemaking questions:

Is it Paris Green or Butter color that you put in the cream and how much? How much salt? Iche kow butter mach von iche was wie.[24]

---

[24] In Pennsylvania German, Samuel wrote "I can make butter, if I know how." Paris Green was the name of an arsenic-based pesticide often used in orchards. Clearly, Samuel was making a joke!

I may strike a plan with John Brandt to fetch you away from Lancaster on the machine on Saturday afternoon. How does this suit you? or are you not tired of Mechanic Grove by that time? I have thought whole around the world for help and everybody seems to be engaged but David Tice and Lizzie Hunnsicher. Now take your choice . . .

It is very warm this evening and there seem to be showers across the mountains. My prayers and my best wishes are with you. Kiss the children for me.

Samuel

(June 7, 1914)

Samuel's familiar gentle humor glows through this letter. He's eager for Fianna to return home although he cloaks it in a gentle query about whether she's tired of Mechanic Grove, the hamlet close to her father's farm. He knows it is hard for her to be so far away from her mother and the Bucher clan with their support and delight in the children, but *he* misses her.

Two weeks after returning home with her children, Fianna gave little Leah back to Mary again. Caring for both Ammon and Leah was more than she could manage. Leah needed to be watched closely. She needed to be carried and have her diapers changed. Even with a "Lizzie" to help, it was too much. The work of a mother and homemaker was enormous in those days: laundry, daily food preparation, gardening and food preservation, cleaning house, tending the chickens or the other animals. I recall my years with two little children the ages of Ammon and Leah. I thought *I* had a challenging life but I had no appreciation of the daily work required from my grandmother a century ago. My privileged late twentieth-century life as a young mother included an electric stove and oven, a washing machine and dryer, an electric vacuum cleaner—to name a few great aids to housekeeping. And, the greatest gift of all, I had good health and energy.

To transfer their daughter to sister Mary's care again, Fianna and Samuel met Mary in Lancaster. The trip from Fianna and Samuel's home to Lancaster included a buggy ride to Lebanon and then the train journey to Lancaster. Since Fianna's sister Leah also lived and worked in Lancaster, the family met both sisters for a visit. Then Fianna kissed her little girl "goodbye" and the family, minus one, returned home.

The letters from Mary to Fianna telling of little Leah's exploits began again:

My dear Sister and Co.

Sunday evening after church. Well I guess you are home by this time. I wonder how you stood it. My baby slept the greater part of the way from Lanc. to Quarryville . . .

When I put those black shoes on her and stood her in the box, she reached down with both hands and took a hold of them and looks at them. I will enclose her pictures. You said you wanted some. How many?

Good night

(June 22, 1914)

Dear Sister,

This is a nice cool Monday morning. I ought to be at the wash tub but my hand has not healed altogether yet. . . . The most Leah walked without help was eight steps. I think she could walk if she knew it. She gets so excited over it and wants to run and then she falls. . . .

(June 29, 1914)

Though Mary didn't sign these letters, I recognize the handwriting and the style, and, as Fianna did when she received them, I read them eagerly. Fianna surely must have been grieved that she couldn't be there to watch Leah learning to walk. How she would have loved to see those initial steps and the plop down on her well-diapered bottom!

Perhaps this longing to *see* her daughter had spurred Fianna and Samuel to have formal photographs taken of the children when they were in Lancaster for the transfer. Since sister Leah lived in the city, she helped them:

Dear sister:-

I guess you are looking for something from me today but you must look a day longer. I was down to see the proof on Friday evening . . . You can not tell much on a proof but they did not move and neither has the tongue out. I am going down on Saturday for them . . .

Lovingly, Leah

(June 23, 1914)

I have a copy of that picture of little Ammon and little Leah. She's right; both of them have their tongues inside their mouths. A week later, she wrote of the printed photos:

... I have Ammon and Leah on the table with me since Saturday and often talk to them but get no answer. I think Leah's is good but wish she would be laughing, am sorry Ammon's is not better. I guess they came a little sooner than you were looking for them, I got them Saturday after-noon and mailed them right away ...

Leah

(July 1, 1914)

Leah and Ammon

Why did Leah feel that Ammon's picture wasn't better? I admit that he is a very solemn little boy in the photo. He focused on being good and remaining perfectly still for the few minutes needed to capture the image. I can imagine the photographer emphasizing to these children how important it was that they didn't move. Ammon's Aunt Leah wanted a big smile for the photograph on her table. Instead, her nephew looked at her intently and seriously as if listening to her speak.

Later in the summer, baby Leah went back to be with her parents for a time because Fianna had special help in the house. Her sister Leah had come to stay with them. Months earlier Leah had written that she would shake the carpets, and Fianna was not to strain herself to try to do it. So she came, and did much more than shake carpets.

Having an energetic, older sister around the house lifted Fianna's spirit and energy. She'd grown up with sisters working together, and now her sister was here to work with her in the garden and the house. I'm sure Leah tackled those carpets with great vigor! Letters Fianna wrote to her mother at this time seem more cheerful and optimistic.

Fianna also wrote of hard things. Samuel's 80-year-old grandfather was dying. Grandfather Joseph Gibbel died on August 12th, 1914, at the Groh/Gibbel farm just outside Fredericksburg. This farmstead had belonged to my family since colonial times, and the old farmhouse with its wide uneven boards, enormous old doors and fireplace was later my childhood home. Samuel's grandfather was a leader in the local church as well as a community leader, one of the early directors of the Fredericksburg National Bank. (Samuel's father was also a director. I wonder if their influence helped Samuel get his bank job. He was quite competent at his work but connections are always helpful.)

Fianna wrote to her mother about their final visit with Grandfather Gibbel:

Dear Mother,

I forgot you were going away till Leah reminded me of it this forenoon. I hope you will get this yet before you go. Whatever you do <u>don't go to Europe just now</u> . . .

I am anxious to hear about Grandfather. He certainly lingers long. We were to see him Sunday evening. He could hardly talk then but seemed to know us. Samuel's parents were there last night and didn't come home . . .

Fianna

(Aug. 12, 1914)

In the letter above, Fianna told her mother that she had forgotten that her parents were traveling. Her father probably had another preaching trip, and her mother was going with him. "Don't go to Europe just now" is mysterious unless one knows what was happening in Europe in August 1914. Germany, having already invaded Belgium and Luxembourg, declared war on France on August 3rd. This led Great Britain to declare war on Germany. It was the last of the toppling dominoes that led to four long years of World War I. The dreadful news of war between the major European countries headlined all the newspapers—including Fianna and Samuel's local paper. On the day Fianna warned her mother against traveling to Europe, big black headlines in their local *Lebanon Daily News* proclaimed "Germans in Heart of Belgium," with additional articles declaring "Big German Army Hurled at France Near Alsace" and "British Warn U.S. of Mines in Sea."

I picture Fianna and Samuel sitting together in the kitchen in the evening, reading the paper and sharing their horror at the outbreak of war. Their church was strongly pacifist, and all war filled them with horror. A war on this scale would inevitably bring great destruction and death. Her message to her mother wasn't a joke; she knew her mother was only traveling with her father for church meetings. She wrote, "don't go to Europe," as a serious acknowledgement of what Europe was facing. Fianna's was a small parochial world, but she also lived within the larger world.

A week later, Fianna's parents were home from their trip, and Fianna wrote them again. This time she wrote about Grandfather's funeral:

Dear Homefolks,

Well, I suppose you are back from your trip by this time . . .

Grandfather's funeral is now a thing of the past. We were so sorry you could not be here. We thought maybe someone else would come. I watched the automobiles on Sunday evening but none stop. Many people asked about you. But of course Grandmother will enjoy your visit more if you can come some other time. It certainly was a large funeral. There were forty some automobiles and I don't know how many teams. Everything was nicely arranged. About sixty people could eat at one time. Grandmother takes it very nicely but she is sick at heart . . .

Little Leah is a pious little girl. Sometimes she kneels at a chair or couch and prays. When she has finished she says "Now." Some people thought she was Aunt Leah's baby yesterday.

Write soon,

Fianna

(Aug. 18, 1914)

Fianna wanted someone from the Bucher family to come to "Grandfather's funeral." Since Samuel's grandfather and her own Grandfather Pfautz were cousins, and both families had deep roots in the Church of the Brethren, she had reason to be hopeful. She sat on the porch on Sunday evening, hoping a car would turn into their driveway and surprise her, but none stopped.

CHAPTER 11

THIS IS TUBERCULOSIS

Though I have no letters sent between Fianna and her Quarryville family for the next two months (September and October 1914), I know what was happening. Fianna's health was worsening. She was losing weight and coughing a lot. She had chest pain, and she often ran a fever. She was fatigued and spent more time resting, unable to be the active homemaker she wanted to be.

A housekeeper named Hannah did much of the physical work and helped care for the children, too. Hannah later helped to hold the little household together when Fianna was at the tuberculosis sanatorium. Increasingly, she became an essential part of the family.

I can't imagine how hard it was for Fianna to feel her health slipping away, and how painful it was for Samuel to watch. He helped her as much as he could, but he also worked in the bank and tended the farm. And in this, the most important thing of all, he couldn't help. He couldn't bring her health back. In spite of taking the medicines the doctor gave her, she wasn't getting better. In fact, she was getting worse.

Finally Fianna and Samuel arranged to see a different doctor. These three letters, to Mary and to her mother, tell the story:

Dear Sister:-

Indeed I have so much to write this morning that I wish you were here and we could talk it all . . .

I wish you could see Leah. She climbs around on the chairs like a monkey. You can imagine how writing goes. I have changed places about half a dozen times since I am writing this . . .

What do you think if I would go to Mont Alto or some sanatorium for a while? We were with Dr. Weiss in Lebanon on Sat. evening. He is one of the hospital doctors. He asked me how long I had this trouble. He was wonderfully surprised that the Doctors didn't advise me to go last spring. He said he has no doubts that I could get well but it would have been better for me to go last spring. He examined my lungs with some kind of an instrument which he put on my bare chest and had tubes to his ears. He could plainly tell by my breathing where the trouble lies. He didn't give me a bit of medicine just advice.

He said the mountain air is much better for treating such cases. We are too low around here. If we know there is anything that will fully cure me we are about ready to make any amount of sacrifice. I know it would cost a lot for young people but what is money compared to health? If I stay at home the Dr. said I should spend about 4/5 of my time in bed. Go to bed at 1pm or when the fever starts up and stay in till the next morning. Have my windows open and then spend the rest of my time outdoors. It might work all right that way but you know how such a thing is almost impossible when you are where there is work right be-

fore. I am not to be at all where a fire is as the fire burns the oxygen out of the air. I am also to take plenty of cod liver oil and not less than 6 raw eggs and 1 qt. milk a day . . .

I told him how I was last spring and how I am now then he said "that shows I have a strong power of resistance." He seemed pleased when I told him I made up my mind to get well.

Now I don't like to tell all this to mother but for my sake I wish she wouldn't worry. I must face the truth and keep up my faith and courage and it will discourage me if she worries. We didn't fully decide as yet as we don't know the particulars as yet. I wish you would write soon and say what you think about it then we will do as we please. (Ha!) . . .

Lovingly,

Fianna

(Nov. 9, 1914)

Dear Sister:-

Your letter came yesterday and I was very, very glad for it. I was looking for one. The exchange told us Q'ville called us on Wed. evening. Samuel and I were in Lebanon and Hannah and the children were alone and the phone was out of fix . . .

We don't like to say anything to Dr. Livingood. We respect him and don't want to hurt his feelings and besides we can't listen on two Drs. of a different opinion. Dr. Weiss seems to understand his business or he wouldn't be used in the Hospital. And he doesn't give me medicine just advice. He goes to a lot of trouble to get information, etc. and he seems concerned about the case . . . There were certain questions to answer such as "Do you own any real estate?" and "What is the monthly income?" Mont Alto is a State Institution and is free. It is all charity work and if we would answer those questions correctly they likely wouldn't take me and we want to abide by the truth . . . The Dr. strongly urged me to go to White Haven . . . He said he is sure I would like it much better there. At Mont Alto you are thrown in with all kinds of people. White Haven is private. Of course we would have to pay there . . . It will take a determination and strong will power to tear away from my home and little ones but I hope it will all be well and turn out for the best.

We had decided to send Leah to you before you wrote. I will feel more at ease that way. Hannah is not so strong. It will make it easier for her and I know my Dolly is in good hands. I don't have all the sewing done yet but I guess I will do Ammon's first and the rest what I can. I can't go away thinking the children don't have warm clothes . . .

Tell mother I want to hear about their trip.

Lovingly,

Fianna

(Nov. 13, 1914)

Dear Mother:-

I just . . . filled out an application for White Haven. We send it to Dr. Weiss then he fills out some more and sends it to Phila. Then they will send us instructions as to what I need, etc. . . . we have decided to come home over Thanksgiving . . .

I expect to go just as soon as we can get ready. If I wouldn't think that I could get well by going I wouldn't do anything like it.

Your cards were appreciated. Ammon's came yesterday. He looked and looked at it till he started to cry and said "I want to go to Grandma's." I promised him we would go.

I guess you are very busy. I wish I could be a help to you. I am looking for a letter again if you are not too busy. My love to all.

> *Fianna*

(Nov. 19, 1914)

At some point, the dreaded word *tuberculosis* had been spoken. I wonder who spoke it. Six months earlier, Dr. Livingood, their first doctor, must have misdiagnosed her illness, and he'd given her useless medicines. By the time they decided to see Dr. Weiss, the disease had advanced. Dr. Weiss listened to her lungs with his stethoscope and knew immediately "where the trouble lies." Fianna had not been examined with a stethoscope before. Stethoscopes weren't a new invention, but Dr. Livingood hadn't used one.

Sadly, even though Dr. Weiss diagnosed correctly and recommended up-to-date treatment, it was no better than Dr. Livingood's treatment. There was no cure for tuberculosis.

The disease of tuberculosis was not even identified as contagious until the late 1800s, and, in 1914, it was still the leading cause of death in the United States. Because its transmission was mysterious, it was feared the more. Few hospitals would admit patients with tuberculosis because of the fear of contagion that surrounded it.

Today we know that the disease is a bacterial infection

that can be carried within the body and lie dormant for many years. Fianna could have been infected as a child, and no one ever knew. Having tuberculosis was not an absolute death sentence; some people did survive. This tenuous hope drove many kinds of treatments even though they were useless.[25]

---

[25]   Barbara Bates, *Bargaining for Life: a Social History of Tuberculosis, 1876-1938* (Philadelphia, University of Pennsylvania Press, 1992) is an excellent source for information on tuberculosis and its treatment at this time, particularly at White Haven.

CHAPTER 12

At White Haven Sanatorium

Fianna and Samuel and their children spent Thanksgiving weekend with her family in Quarryville. What a mix of emotions Fianna must have felt during this precious time together. There were surely moments of fear that she might never return to her childhood home again, but they mingled with the hope and faith that she *would* recover at White Haven. I suspect she only shared her hope, especially since she didn't want her mother to worry and be afraid for her. There was sadness in giving little Leah to Mary again and gladness that Mary wanted her. There was surely laughter and humor within this lively gathering that brought her joy. And deepest of all flowed a gratitude and love for her family, and for all their support, love, and prayers. She had so much to be grateful for!

A few days later, Fianna, Samuel, and Ammon set out on the long train trip to White Haven Sanatorium. Fianna's trunk had been packed. Samuel carried the hand luggage, and Fianna held Ammon's hand. The adventure had begun.

White Haven Sanatorium, perched high in the mountains of northeastern Pennsylvania, had been founded as a center for tubercular patients. It was connected to a hospital in Philadelphia that also focused on such patients, and both were supported by a charitable fund called the Free Hospital for Poor Consumptives. Physicians associated with Thomas Jefferson University in Philadelphia provided patient care. Most of the staff were survivors of tuberculosis and, therefore, weren't afraid of being infected with it.[26]

White Haven Tuberculosis Sanatorium, 1914

In old pictures, White Haven looks a little like a college campus. It was a collection of large brick buildings called "Cottages" although pictures show them to be more like dormitories. Fianna lived in Rose Cottage.

White Haven's treatment included its location: high altitude and fresh air. Cold dry air was thought to be therapeutic.

[26] Bates, *Bargaining for Life;* also, Richard Sucre, "The Great White Plague: The Culture of Death and the Tuberculosis Sanatorium," http://www.faculty.virginia.edu/blueridgesanatorium/death.htm (accessed 10/15/2019).

To fully experience fresh air, the windows were kept open year round. The patients slept outdoors on wide, covered balconies even in wintertime. White Haven's isolated location also protected the general population from infection.

Fianna had never been so distant from home as this. She was far away from her Pennsylvania German farming community, far away from her close-knit church community, and far away from her family. She was surrounded by people from many nationalities and religions, most of them from cities. Her fellow patients were people whose lives were very different from hers. White Haven was as strange to her as it was to patients coming from New York City to live in the mountains.

Fianna's first letters describe the shape of her life at White Haven. She expected her family would pass them around since they were all very eager to hear news from her:

Dear Mother & all:-

We came here yesterday about 2:30 pm. This is a beautiful place and everybody is kind so after I am used to it I think I will like it fine.

I just had dinner. Had bread, butter, soup, potatoes, baked beans, meat about four times as much as I could eat. Also stewed apples and coffee. The other meals are made up of raw eggs, milk, and fruit. I took three eggs this forenoon and am expected to take 3 qts. of milk a day.

I hope you can arrange to come sometime. I know you will like the place and I will be so glad to see some one. We have plenty of bed covers. No comforts [comforters]. Wool blankets and a lot of them. The nurse said I could have more if I wanted it. I am in bed of course. My trunk isn't here yet. I think they are slow in getting it and when it does come they don't bring it in here. The nurses get for me what I need. The nurses got a nightgown for me. And I have a heavy bed blanket over my shoulders & chest. I am indoors yet but I suppose they will put me out on the balcony too after a while. Most of them are out there. It is fixed up with windows so it can be opened all around. My room is open too.

My day nurse had tuberculosis and is well now. A patient told me that most of the people that work here had it at one time.

Most of the patients are in a good humor. That makes it cheerful. I hope nothing will happen that I can't stay here till I am fully recovered . . .

We took Ammon along yesterday. He was awake and we were afraid he'd cry. When they left he waved his hand and was in a good humor. The people here thought I had such a sweet little boy. When you come I would like to see baby Leah in case some one comes with you.

I don't think I ever saw mountains till yesterday. I almost feel as though I were nearer heaven than at home. We are up so high.

Write soon.

Fianna

(Dec. 3, 1914)

Dear Sister [Leah] :-

I wrote a letter home on Thurs. I don't know if they sent it to you or not. So this time I'll write to you and let you send it home.

I had a letter from Samuel on Friday and the New Era [Lancaster newspaper]. Yesterday I had a card from Mary. You can't imagine how much good it does me. I am kept in bed in-doors yet. There are two double doors leading out on the balcony which are open.

There are eight doctors to this institution called chiefs. They come from Phila. every two weeks. Dr. Landis is my chief and will be here next Sat. I don't suppose I'll get my full treat-ments till he was here . . . There are 135-140 patients. There are lots of buildings and beautiful, too. Last evening the nurse showed me a building farther up than we are. She said "There are the dying cases." I said "I am glad they are so far away." I think it would be discouraging to see so much. One girl told me a woman died in this building since she is here. And she just made fun of it. I think I never saw a happier set of afflicted people than here. There are nine patients on this floor. That's about all I get to see. It is pitiful to hear some of them coughing but I am get-ting used to it . . . Someone told me that everybody here has had tuberculosis but the Dr. that is here now and the head nurse.

In general I like it very well but I must fight against being homesick for the children. And it seems I can't get used to the milk and eggs. They make me so sick. At first I got diarrhea. The Dr. gave me some different medicine. The diarrhea stopped but this forenoon I had a vomiting spell. I was to take 6 eggs and 12 big glasses of milk. They changed it to 4 and 10 now. But I can hardly stomach that. I hope I will soon get used to it. I get discouraged when I feel so sick. We get more than we can eat at dinner time . . .

The nurses are very kind. I didn't get one cross word yet. But when you want something you must ask and ask for it till you get it. I didn't get anything out of my trunk till Friday. You see they have the trunks in another building and the nurse gets what you need. If she left the trunk as upside-down as she brought some of my things, I'm afraid my dresses and things are a sight . . . When she went to my trunk the first time I gave her a list but forgot some things. After she came back I told her I would have liked to have my Bible and some other things. She said she saw a Bible but didn't know if I wanted it. When she went the second time she didn't bring my Bible so I guess this week sometime I will muster up courage and ask for my Bible and some other things.

I think the nurses are all Catholic. But they are very nice. Nearly all the patients on this floor are Protestants. The head nurse in this building thought I am a real Quakeress. Another one asked if my little cap keeps my head warm. When I said No, she asked if I have it to keep my hair up. She looked very much surprised when I told her all the sisters in our church wear it.

I wish you could come to see me sometime. But I won't urge you if you can't. I believe it is beautiful here in summertime . . .

I wish I had something good to read. There are some old papers here but there isn't much in them I like very well. Do you think it would hurt me to read "The White Slave Traffic"? When I have good reading I can easily pass the time. Sometimes when I feel discouraged I gain courage when I think some people are thinking of and praying for me . . .

I guess I will stop and rest a while and maybe hunt something to read. I am half sitting in bed with my bathrobe and my shawl on. I am warm. Some of the patients don't have any underclothes on. I can't see how they keep warm. Write me a big letter soon. I hope this is interesting to you. I wrote so much.

Lovingly,

Fianna

Monday morning.
P.S. *Your letter just came. I was very glad for it. Samuel also sent me a clock. That is lots of company. I never knew what time it was . . .*

You wrote you are anxious to know what they think of me here. The patients are not allowed to know anything but what they find out on the sly. But Samuel wrote me that the Dr. told him "There are lots of people walking around enjoying good health that have much larger cavities in their lungs than I do." If I improve I don't expect to get away in three months. I hope I can get used to the diet. Just now I either vomit or have diarrhea and that weakens me so. I have sweats every night . . .

You said you are glad the home leaving is over. Well, I didn't mind leaving the house & furniture but it took me to the test when Samuel and Ammon left here. I am glad we took Ammon along. He enjoyed it so much. He fairly screamed when he would see a high mountain. He certainly saw mountains. Samuel said on the way home he danced every time they took the train. It was about 11:30 when they came home.

. . . Samuel expects to come up here on Christmas.

(received Dec. 8, 1914)

Fianna's family was anxious and full of questions about her new life. I imagine Samuel telephoned and wrote letters to tell them what he could, but Fianna's letters provided the most complete picture of White Haven and what it was like to live there. She was a patient in a large institution with strict procedures and rules. To receive things from her trunk, the belongings she had carefully chosen and packed, she had to ask repeatedly for them. She needed to muster up her courage again and again. Being a new patient was intimidating, but her fellow patients and nurses were kind. Slowly she was finding her way.

All the patients followed the raw eggs and milk diet that Fianna described. Unfortunately, the quantity of milk and eggs that Fianna was forced to ingest made her ill. During her ten weeks at White Haven, digestion issues from this diet continued to weaken her.

Fianna was writing about her experiences of settling in, but homesickness and longing for family kept slipping into the letters. White Haven was so far from home. And no one knew the familiar hills and farms of Lancaster and Lebanon Counties. No one knew of her Brethren world. They wondered if she wore the simple netted prayer covering for warmth. Her plain dress labeled her a "Quakeress."

No, Fianna, you were not a Quakeress, but you have descendants who are! I am a Quaker, and so are your two great-granddaughters and four great-great-granddaughters.

After two weeks at White Haven, Fianna seemed to have settled into the Sanatorium's routine. She wrote quite cheerfully to her mother a week before Christmas:

My dear Mother:-
Your two letters came this evening in company with four others. Don't say that it didn't make me happy. I appreciate them all so much but I certainly won't undertake to answer them all. It is best for me in bed. I think they will keep me there till my temperature stops going up in the afternoon . . .

Leah made me a pair of beautiful, warm bed socks and sent them for a Christmas present. She made them double out of light blue eiderdown and put light blue ribbon ties on them. I had them on last night. My feet felt so nice and warm all night. This morning the nurse brought my comfort [comforter]. Now I am fixed. I always take the hot water bag along to bed. My! but my nose gets cold and that is the one thing I daren't cover up.

The Dr. told me I gained 2 1/2 lbs. since I am here. That's doing something for being sick in my stomach nearly all the time. But when dinner time comes I can usually eat better than the other patients.

I had to laugh when the stamps dropped out of your letter. Samuel also sent me 25. It looks as though I had been hinting . . . They are hard to get here. You see we can't go after them.

You needn't be jealous of Samuel's parents. They weren't here yet and if they do come it will be Samuel's doings. He tried to get them to come last week . . .

Yes, we have snow. I hear sleigh bells all around during the day.

. . . You may bring me something good to eat . . . Of course the rules say not but lots of the other patients get little things that way. I asked Samuel to bring pretzels along. When you come maybe you can bring some good butter bread and dried beef or something like that . . . I know it won't hurt me to eat a little with my milk.

Most of the management and lots of patients are Catholic. Tomorrow is Friday. We have fish every Friday as Catholics don't eat meat then. There is a little chapel in the main building. Sometimes there are Catholic services. Sunday is like any other day unless we try to feel different . . .

I ought to write to my Samuel too. Just one week till he comes.

   Much love,

      Fianna

(Dec. 17, 1914)

Fianna wanted to keep her mother from worrying. She tried to write cheerfully even through her own struggles, and she focused on all she was grateful for. There were so many reminders of family love around her. There were bed slippers and comforter and Samuel's clock and extra stamps! And special foods from home have always carried love to those far away.

CHAPTER 13

Mail Call

Having a large family and a close-knit faith community meant letters and cards poured into White Haven for Fianna. One week she received 15 letters. She didn't attempt to respond to everyone, but knowing that so many others were thinking of her gave her a tremendous lift. And she could read them over and over again—much better reading than *The White Slave Traffic!*

Mail and visitors were especially important because there was nothing else to do. There was no activities director to plan activities and help the patients pass the time. There was no book cart with reading material. Fianna was not alone in depending on letters. White Haven was very isolated, and the tubercular patients from New York City or Philadelphia didn't receive many visitors either. Mail call was a true highlight for Fianna and her fellow patients.

For the families and friends left behind, news from Fianna was equally longed for. The Buchers and Meyers passed all her letters around. Referring to a card that Fianna had sent to their housekeeper Hannah, Samuel wrote to his wife:

Hannah's card was a satisfaction. I showed it to the boys at the bank, to father and boys over home, to Levi's, and at the teachers' training class, etc. Hannah seemed glad of it also.

(Dec. 14, 1914)

I love my grandfather Samuel's sly sense of humor. Surely it was a joy in their marriage that they laughed together at some silly things. Samuel's letters included news from church and family, and he always told about the children:

My dear Fianna:-

Your letter states that you are glad for letters and you can rest assured that you are not the only one . . .

You mentioned the Lanc. paper. I used to depend upon you to give me the Lanc. Co. news and now if you don't mind I glance over it and send it with the next mail. If you have a place to store The Messenger [church magazine] *I will mail it every Monday . . .*

Oh, yes, Ammon does not forget you. He often talks of you but we tell him that you want to get well and then he is satisfied. He says, "Mamma is at White Haven," "Mamma will stay there a while," "Mamma wants to get well."

I told him that we will go to see Mamma on Xmas. That makes him laugh & jump . . .

I had a letter from Mary. She is pleased with Leah. She is well and happy not knowing how we are scattered. I hope & pray that she may be well. I feel that she is well cared for. Mary says that Mother furnished paper and envelopes to write to you and me but not for any other purpose.

Miriam Fausnacht was going to write. If she uses as little common sense in writing as in speaking, let me suggest that you burn her letter before you read it, or make it like the man who was kicked by a mule who said he was considering the source . . .

> *Samuel*

> (Dec. 14, 1914)

I wonder what Fianna did with Miriam Fausnacht's letter if she received one. Fianna's family often gave the White Haven address to friends who promised to write. There was much love sent her way; many prayers offered for her healing. Even if letters simply told familiar church and home news, the time and effort given to the writing strengthened her for White Haven living. Of course, Miriam's letter may have been an exception.

As the days passed, Fianna learned to know other patients in Rose Cottage. Since the woman in the next bed to hers couldn't read or write, Fianna offered to write a letter for her. It made her feel good to be helpful, but, as she wrote to Leah, it was harder to receive help:

My dear Sister:-

I just finished writing a letter for next door neighbor. She is bedfast. She is a Jew and can't read or write. I wrote to her husband . . . I was very glad for your letter and also got one from Samuel and one from home. You don't know how I enjoy that. I am almost afraid or I mean I don't like to ask you for anything anymore. You want to do it all for nothing. You are so kind to us.

I hope you will or do realize a blessing through it. I am sure my happiness is greatly increased by it . . .

Fianna

(Dec. 15, 1914)

Sister Leah was a housekeeper for a wealthy Lancaster family. Housekeepers were not well paid, and Leah didn't have much money to spend on gifts. She gave her time instead, making warm bed socks for a Christmas present for Fianna and decorating them with ribbons. And, remembering little Ammon at home alone with his father, she frequently purchased postcards to send to him. Leah responded to Fianna's concern that she was giving too much:

My dear sister:-

. . . As usual I wonder how you are . . . I was very glad to know that you can return the milk better. I hope your bowels and stomach will soon get better, it is bad enough to lie around and to feel good but it is hard to feel badly all the time. I don't wounder you felt blue the other Saturday night but I am glad that you had something that amused you and if the poor cats were in trouble you gave us some cheer by desiring to share your milk and eggs with the old black cat . . .

All I care for most just now is that you will be able to return home sooner than you think. "the eyes of the Lord are over the righteous and his ears are open unto their prayers." [27] *This scripture was in my mind a good bit last week and I wondered if*

---

[27]   1st Peter 3:12.

it is an answer to prayer. I am glad Samuel is coming to see you at Xmas. I sent a card to Ammon last week, it had a bird on. I thought he would like it . . .

I am glad you like them (bed socks). I did want to please you. Some time when you write tell me how they fit . . . then if I might want to make another pair I would know where to improve them . . . you said on one of your cards that you are almost afraid to ask me to do anything as I want to do it all for nothing and that you hope I do realize a blessing and that your happiness is greatly increased. Well that is all I want. I like to do all I can to make you happy and you see I am not rich but I am blessed with health that I can work and maybe the time will come that I am sick and you are well. Then you see I might depend on you for even more than I am doing for you so we'll help each other along. You see I do not have a good man like you do when I get sick . . .

. . . so now I can not come to you to bring sunshine but if there is anything you want don't hesitate to ask . . .

With much Love,

Leah

(Dec. 21, 1914)

How could Leah *not* want to do everything she could for her little sister? When Fianna was a small child, Leah had carried her around, played with her, and taught her. She watched her grow up, fall in love, and get married. She didn't have the money to go and visit her sister, but she prayed for her and wrote to her. And she anguished over her.

Letters from sister Mary often included stories about Fianna's little Leah. Besides having the pet name "Dolly," she had also earned the nickname "Little Mischief." Mary's letters were often like a diary with pages recording farm, home, church, and Dolly activities of the week:

My dear Sister:-

I received your letter today. We all read it around here now . . . Phares just now got done reading your letter. He said he would try and learn all about Russia he could . . .

I feel sorry for you that they put you down among these fariners [foreigners]. But they are human and have souls too. If they treat you alright and give you the proper attention, try and become reconciled . . .

What do you keep in your wardrobes if you are not allowed to have your trunks? I'd ask for my dresses and hang them in the wardrobe. What do you keep in your bureau? Did you get your Bible? If you did not we will send you one. Mother said if Samuel comes on Christmas, they would wait and come later . . .

Dec. 12. Another day is gone. I have nothing of importance to write tonight. The telephone is out of fix nearly all week . . . My Dolly almost scared me this evening after she was in bed. She fussed and then cried. It seemed as though something hurt her. I asked her if she was wet, if she wanted a dry didie [diaper] on, then she looked pleased. I put one on her and powdered her good, and when I was done she laughed and said "Now." Then everything was alright.

Dec. 13 . . . This evening Dolly had a hollering spell in church and the more I tried to quiet her the harder she laughed. So I just left her sit on the bench and folded my hands on my lap, and paid no attention to her. Then she got on my lap and I hardly could look at her and hardly dared to touch her till she laughed. Finally I got her attention on some play thing . . .

(Dec. 10-13, 1914)

In this letter, Mary was responding to the news that Fianna had been moved to another floor. There were more immigrants from the cities, strange "fariners" to Mary. If Phares had visited, he could have learned a lot about Russia.

Although Fianna tried to keep a cheerful attitude, it wasn't easy. She had to begin over again in another area of Rose Cottage. She needed to learn about her new roommates, their names and stories, and to discover who was companionable and who wasn't. Again she had to answer questions about herself. Why was she wearing the "little cap"? Did the farm she came from have cows and chickens? Had there been no other problems, I think she could have adjusted to the new floor quickly. But other difficulties were crushing her spirit.

CHAPTER 14

CHRISTMAS TROUBLES
AT WHITE HAVEN

Christmas was coming, and Fianna was counting the days until Samuel and Ammon would come again. She tried to be cheerful, but she was homesick for them and for the familiar faith community that sustained her. It was painful to be surrounded by people who didn't care about those things most dear to her heart. It was also painful to be so powerless, to feel that the medical professionals weren't really listening to her. In this letter, Fianna poured her heart out to Samuel:

My dear Samuel:-

This is a most beautiful sunshiny Sunday. I thought about you and Ammon and Hannah. I imagined Ammon with his little red suit on sitting with you in church like a good boy. And this afternoon you are in S.S. I hope you may have a good season of Bible Study. My! but how you hunger for such occasions when you are entirely cut away from them! But if it be the Lord's will I can almost make any amount of sacrifice. I try "in whatsoever state I am therewith to be content." [28]

---

[28] Philippians 4:11.

This noon the undertaker was on the hill twice inside of an hour. He took another one out of this building . . .

I can hardly wait till Christmas. I shall try to find out about the hotel before I send this. Visitors come any time they feel like it forenoon or afternoon. When you come you might ask in the main building. But I have seen that when visitors once know where the patients are they walk right in . . .

It is just 6:25 P.M. now. I just finished my 6 o'clock diet. I took an egg, one glass milk and some apple sauce. I cut my diet down from 10-8 glasses of milk . . . Eight glasses make me sick and I just have to force it down. I don't like to complain to you all the time. I would rather tell you all pleasant things. Don't get discouraged if I tell you I don't feel so well as I did when I came. But I hope for better things. You see my stomach and bowels are sickened all the time from the eggs & milk. I think my stomach would be better if I wouldn't force it so. At dinner time I can eat well and by 4 o'clock I am hungry again. But then I feel miserable the rest of the evening . . . My temperature was up to 102° last evening . . .

I was disappointed a little in Dr. Webster. He used to say "It takes patience." and "Oh! Lord!" or something similar. You have no idea how little some people think of using God's name in vain . . . Well, Dr. Landis told him to change my medicine if my bowels don't get better. Well, when I had that spell this week I had a pain in my side I could hardly walk. I told him in the evening then he said "If it isn't better tomorrow we'll change your medicine." He didn't come around till late next evening then he only said "It's too bad." Well such things disgust me. He just left me suffer on. He left this place yesterday for good. Now we have a new Doctor. I saw him this evening. He listened to it all and asked me a lot of questions and looked over my chart. He prescribed different medicine and I really felt better when I saw he took interest. Some of the other patients said I must make it really worse than it is to attract attention or else tell you to speak for me. They saw I was being neglected. They certainly stick to dying patients but when you are up and around you must fight for your rights . . .

Well, such things we must meet and I can put up with it if only I am privileged to get well. I long for the time to be with my dear ones again. Pray for me that I may bear up under it all. I often pray for you all that all may be well with you. And I have that abiding trust in Him that I feel all is well . . .

<u>Monday morning.</u>

I slept fine under the snow last night. Our beds were white and I sweated under it. Early this morning the night nurse came in and closed most of the windows and shook the snow off our beds . . .

My room-mate just told me on Christmas week the patients are allowed to get any kind of packages with edibles, etc. She said some get boxes of chicken, etc. They are not near so strict as the rules say . . .

Lovingly,

Fianna

P.S. I talked with our good nurse about a boarding place. She said there is a lady that lives at the foot of the hill who takes boarders during Christmas week . . .

(dated Dec. 18, 1914)

What a painful letter for Samuel to receive! Fianna wasn't getting better. In fact, she was worse. The treatment itself was weakening her, and sometimes she was simply neglected. She was so far away, and he was so helpless. I can see him kneeling down in the evening after Ammon was in bed and praying fervently for the recovery of his Fianna. Faith like Fianna and Samuel's was buttressed by prayer. They prayed not only for their deepest desire, Fianna's recovery, but also for the strength to bear whatever was to come. And they prayed constantly.

Theirs was no blind, easy faith, the kind of faith that says if you pray enough you will be healed. They lived with the mystery of good people dying, and they knew it could happen to Fianna. She was surrounded by death. The undertakers came frequently to White Haven. She even observed that, if she were dying, the doctors would pay more attention to her. Her roommates suggested she pretend to have more pain than she did, but I doubt that she followed their advice. She could not lie.

But Christmas was coming soon. On Christmas Day Samuel and little Ammon would take the train to White Haven to visit Fianna. They would stay overnight in the house at the foot of the hill. They were Fianna's first visitors, and they could hardly wait to see her again. Even family members who couldn't visit Fianna rejoiced with them. Ammon's Aunt Leah sent him an embossed postcard decorated with a bright Christmas robin and holly:

Dear Ammon:-

I saw this pretty card in the store and I thought Ammon must have it. I wounder if you are going to see Mamma next week. I guess she will laugh when Ammon come.

with love from Aunt Leah

(Dec. 18, 1914)

Ammon's note to his Mamma, as dictated to his Papa, told her how eager he was to see her. Though it was only three weeks since she'd gone to White Haven, it was a very long time for the little boy:

My dear Mamma:-

I got a nice card from Aunt Leah and one from baby Leah and one from you. I see the chickens. Do you feed those nice chickens?

I am coming to see you on Xmas. Papa will go with me. I love you Mamma. I want you to get well. I can run and play. I make bath tubs and houses and engines.

Now I am done. Send me a card again.

Ammon

(Dec. 20, 1914)

Fianna wrote back to her son:

My dear little boy:-

I got your letter today and was very glad for it. Do you see the little birds on this card? What do the birds say? Do you see the house and trees? How is Aunt Hannah?

Mamma

Fianna's postcard with bluebirds sent to Ammon

Across the miles this Mamma was trying to stay close to her son. She chose a wintry landscape picture with bluebirds and sent the postcard with questions for him. I imagine Samuel reading the card to the curious little three year old after he came home from the bank. Together they counted the bluebirds and tried to imagine what they were saying. Mamma's presence was strongly felt in the farmhouse that evening.

This was the golden age of postcards. Often Christmas postcards were sent to friends and family instead of cards within an envelope. Ammon had begun a postcard collection, inserting the cards into a special book his Bucher grandmother had given him. These cards from his aunt Leah and his mother were proudly displayed among them.

The Brethren celebration of Christmas was muted in comparison with the culture around them, but it was still a special celebration. Friends and family would gather for a festive Christmas dinner and perhaps an exchange of small gifts. Fianna wistfully thought of what she would be missing.

A few days before Christmas, Fianna wrote to her sister Mary:

> *My roommate told me that during Christmas week the patients are allowed to receive any kind of packages with things to eat in or anything up to New Year. Does that sound like hinting? I wish I could be with you Christmas but I hope to be happy here, too.*
>
> (Dec. 21, 1914)

Since she had already told Mary that she was "so hungry for something salty," I hope Mary took the hint and sent a box of good Lancaster County pretzels!

In the same letter, Fianna wrote of her longing for little Leah, whom she would not see:

> *Well, baby Leah certainly isn't losing any of her mischief and I hope she won't till I see her again. She wouldn't be natural as mischief seems to be a part of her element. I imagine I can see her naughty brown eyes now and I feel like taking her in my arms and give her a hug. I hope she will learn to be better in church . . . .*
>
> (Dec. 21, 1914)

Samuel and Ammon's visit on Christmas Day was surely the best present Fianna could have received even if baby

Leah wasn't going to be there. They took the early 5:40 a.m. train from Lebanon so they could arrive at White Haven early enough to surprise Fianna. They were there three hours before she expected them!

I imagine that Ammon, seeing his mother, broke into a run and threw his arms around her. I can see her bending down to hug him, and Samuel smiling happily at the sight. Fianna was probably not strong enough to walk around the grounds, but perhaps they ventured outside. After all, it couldn't be colder than it was at night when she was *sleeping* out on the balcony. I wonder what gifts Samuel brought her and what favorite foods she received.

Many families would have come together at the Sanatorium for Christmas. In spite of the possibility of death that hovered invisibly around them, there was a great deal of happiness in the air. And what a medley of foods was brought together from the different cultures—baklava and strudel and pastas, and maybe borscht and blini from Russia. What a medley of languages wove around the little Meyer family as they spent those precious hours together.

What did they talk about as Ammon climbed on his mother's lap, and she laughed and held his hand? Did they talk about the farm and the chickens? Did Fianna ask how Grandma Gibbel was doing since Grandpa Gibbel died? They certainly shared news about little Leah and the rest of the family. And they must have talked about church activities, who preached on Sunday and who was there for Bible Study. Though their letters had contained daily news, it was a joy to talk about it face to face once more.

But it was not all joy during those days.

After he returned home, Samuel wrote a long letter to Fianna's family, telling them about this Christmas trip:

Dear Homefolks:-

. . . Well, she looks better was my first impression. Sleeping outdoors makes her color better. Her room mate is a Russian woman. Her next door neighbors are a Jewish woman and a Polish woman. Fianna has not yet fallen in love with milk and eggs as a diet four times a day. She has temperatures and more or less night sweats and looseness of the bowels.

She said that the nurses neglect her in some things. She had medicine prescribed by Dr. Hill Sunday before I came and did not get it until this Sunday. etc. I saw that her complaints were reasonable and not only notion. So I tried to find out where the trouble lies or who was to blame. I could not go away until these things were corrected. We watched patiently all day but no new medicine came. This medicine was especially for the bowels. There was no change Saturday. So I approached the junior nurse about it . . .

Samuel was determined to untangle the system, to discover why Fianna was neglected, and who was responsible to carry out doctor's orders. Not surprisingly, the junior nurse passed the responsibility on to the senior nurse:

So I went to this Senior nurse who has charge of the whole of Rose Cottage and said, "As I understand some special medicine was prescribed last Sunday and my wife does not have it to this day and I feel that she is being neglected."

Go, Grandfather! A fierce Christmas knight had come to defend Fianna! A determined and tenacious advocate in plain black suit and a strong Pennsylvania German flavor to his speech would have surprised the staff. He didn't raise his voice in anger. His was a quiet stubbornness; he simply didn't go away:

She tried to cover it up by a flood of nice words. But this did not bring a remedy. I knew that this must be reported higher up. I now heard that Dr. Landis was not coming until Sunday and I decided to stay to see him. I talked the matter over with a few who boarded and lodged where I did.

The advice Samuel received from other lodgers was mixed: Tell the Superintendent, tell Dr. Armstrong, tell Dr. Landis. But they told him not to trust the staff who were primarily Catholic. I wonder if there was mistrust between Catholics and Protestants at this time. Or perhaps Samuel had his own prejudices about the unfamiliar Catholic world. Among the plain Brethren, ornate Catholic churches, crucifixes, and Latin masses were a little suspect. It was almost as foreign to Samuel as were the eastern European immigrants in Rose Cottage. He decided to seek out Dr. Armstrong, one of the hospital chiefs, who was Protestant:

I decided to see him if possible. Dr. Armstrong has had tuberculosis himself. He is cured and lives in the town of White Haven . . . He is one of two men who have charge of the institution. Ammon & I went to see him Sunday morning and talked with him the best part of an hour. He said, "We did not consider her a hopeless case," "I am sure that Senior nurse lied herself out of a similar complaint yesterday," "It is too bad Catholic sentiment gets so strong here." "I will give her my personal attention," "I would advise you to stay until Dr. Landis comes."

... I decided to stay until I see Dr. Landis and if I had to wait a few days longer. I telegraphed home that I was not coming before Monday night.

Monday morning Dr. Armstrong came. He spoke <u>sharp</u> to those nurses. They hate him. The head nurse came into our room and said she didn't know there was any dissatisfaction. We said we had reported it to the junior and then to the senior nurse but in vain. She and Fianna then got words and she got hot. Fianna kept cool for she had the points and I guess a whole lot more brains than the nurse thought. The nurse finally yielded her ground by saying that the druggist must have forgotten to prepare that one kind of medicine.

I told her again that I felt that my wife was being neglected and that I was not going away until these things were all corrected until Dr. Landis arrives. By this time she fairly trembled. I had a notion to ask her whether she often gets hot with her patients but she was too humble by this time . . .

And so Samuel waited, adamantly determined to see Dr. Landis. He wrote that the nurses hinted that he might miss his train because Dr. Landis was likely to be late:

I was bound to see Dr. Landis. He came at 4:30 and our next train and last train was due 5:26.

Now Dr. Landis is a very common man. He came into Fianna's room with his hat on and whistled while he looked over her chart . . . I asked to see him privately and I did. He took the same train we did and I got to talk with him at some length. He said to make a long story short, "We must wait and see." He wants her to keep in quiet and in bed to reduce her temperature. I told her that we don't want to worry her for long letters . . .

Dr. Armstrong promised me & Fianna that she would not be moved again unless he was called for and Fianna would give her consent. This was a satisfaction to both of us.

I never imagined my gentle, mild-mannered grandfather as a warrior battling a dragon on behalf of his lady but that's what he was about. The institutional dragon, the dragon of staff indifference, and the dragon of tuberculosis—he battled them all for his Fianna.

Besides fighting dragons, Samuel also needed to care for Ammon. The wide-eyed little boy was with him all the time. He was present for the conflicts with staff, and he went with his father to Dr. Armstrong's house. I wonder what he understood about all of it. I imagine Fianna reading a storybook to him or perhaps sitting with him and watching him play with a toy on the floor. At night in the house at the foot of the hill, Samuel tucked him in bed, and then he knelt down by his own bed and prayed.

Samuel ended this long letter by writing about Ammon:

I took Ammon down the hill on my back and went up every morning with milk teams.

Fianna was cheerful when I left. She was at the door and waved good-bye.

Samuel

(Dec. 30, 1914)

This long letter wasn't the only letter Samuel wrote about his Christmas visit to White Haven. His second letter was marked "Private" and was addressed to Mary and her husband. This news was even harder to share. He didn't want Fianna's parents to be grieved, but he had to tell someone:

Phares & Mary:-

I want you to read the letter I wrote to [Fianna's] father that contains the best and this one the worst . . .

I think Fianna <u>looks better.</u> She may feel a little bit weak but she is in bed most of the time. She said if we see that she is sinking we should not let her there. I tried to encourage her and increase her willpower to get well.

Dr. Landis said to me privately "She is a very sick woman." "The recovery depends on how long she keeps up that temperature." etc. . . . She does not know the statements made above.

Samuel's letter describing his Christmas visit

Dr. Armstrong made an expression that shocked me. He said, "If that diarrhea is tubercular she cannot recover." I am consoling myself that it is not . . .

I walked out one day and back of the Sanatorium I found a path leading to the top of the mountain which overlooks the highest hills far and wide. When I came to the top, the occasion and quietude moved me to kneel on the pure snow and kneel and pray earnestly for the recovery of her who brought so much sunshine in my life. What more can I do than to pray Lord I believe help thou mine unbelief.

It is too bad I have to send you such sad news but I only hope and pray that I don't need to send you anything worse.

I often think of Leah. I know she is well taken care of. How can I ever pay the debt of kindness I owe you?

Samuel

(Dec. 30, 1914)

How did Mary and Phares feel on receiving this letter? The doctors viewed Fianna's condition as grave and warned Samuel that she might not recover. Did Mary and Phares share this letter with the rest of the family? I think not. I am sure they, like Samuel, knelt and prayed for Fianna, and for Samuel, too, in his lonely pain.

Fianna's condition may have been critical, but she didn't know it. After those few wonderful days when Samuel and Ammon were with her, she was probably given more respect and less neglect. After all, she had a stubborn, black-suited knight, as well as the all-powerful doctors, on her side.

Being with Samuel and Ammon for several days made

it even harder to be far from her family. Fianna sent cheerful New Year's postcards to her children. Ammon's card showed a little boy and a smaller girl standing in the snow and ringing a doorbell. Fianna wrote, "I guess this is Ammon and Leah on this card. Don't you think so?" To Leah, she wrote, "My dear Little Girl, I am glad to hear you feel so well at home with Aunt Mary . . . a hug and a kiss to you, Dolly."

Fianna's postcard sent to Ammon

CHAPTER 15

Receiving the
White Haven Treatment

In 21st-century United States, tuberculosis often seems like a disease from the past. Although it still exists, it is comparatively rare. The truth is that about 9,000 new cases were reported in the United States in 2018. We know it is curable with antibiotics. It is still, however, a leading cause of death around the world. In 2015, there were over a million and a half tuberculosis-related deaths. Treatment of tuberculosis remains complex, even with the best 21st-century medicine. It requires many months of carefully combined antibiotics before the patient has fully recovered, much longer than any other bacterial infections.

True treatment of tuberculosis depends on antibiotics, and antibiotics did not enter the medical scene until the 1940s. Before then, ideas of treatment had varied widely through the centuries. Medical quackery in every generation claimed certain potions would provide "A Complete Cure!" In the 1800s, George Bernard Shaw described the best that Victorian England had to offer the tuberculosis patient as "a commercial system of quackery and poison." But some patients did survive the disease. Their experiences fed a desperate hope for any treatment that would increase the chance of survival.[29]

By the time of tuberculosis sanatoriums in the late 1800s, the medical emphasis was not on an interventionist treatment, such as antibiotics would eventually provide, but on helping one's body resist the disease and heal itself. The emphasis was on strengthening the body's own immune response. This was the approach Fianna found at White Haven.

Treatment was three-pronged. Taking cold, fresh mountain air into one's lungs was essential to clear and strengthen the lungs. Secondly, patients needed to ingest large quantities of eggs and milk because they were considered highly nutritious and easily digested. The third essential was bed rest, particularly if the patient had an elevated temperature. This was state-of-the-art medicine in 1915, and Fianna received all of it.

Dr. Laurence C. Flick, founder of White Haven and an important leader in the study and treatment of tuberculosis, contributed a chapter on tuberculosis treatment to a 1909 book titled *Household Companion: The Family Doctor.* There he described the importance of these three elements. He wrote:

> A tuberculosis subject should sit in the open air all
> day while under treatment and should sleep in a room
> with the windows open on two sides, unless he can do

---

[29] M. D. Iseman, "Tuberculosis Therapy: Past Present and Future," *European Respiratory Journal,* 2002, https://erj.ersjournals.com/content/20/36_suppl/87S (accessed 10/15/2019); also, Talwar A., Tsang C. A., Price S. F., et al. "Tuberculosis—United States," 2018. *MMWR Morb Mortal Wkly Rep* 2019; 68:257-262. https://www.cdc.gov/features/burden-tb-us/index.html (accessed 10/15/19).

what is better still, sleep out of doors . . . Sun and air should be allowed free access to every sleeping room.[30]

The patients at White Haven slept out on the balconies in wintertime, even when their beds were covered by snow. The balconies of these buildings were like big rooms with large open windows on three sides. Fianna wrote to Mary:

The other night I was disturbed a little by the snow coming in my face. I wasn't cold but it tickled so and I kept wiping it and couldn't sleep. I felt my pillow was all snowy both sides of my head. The night nurse came and pulled my bed around after a while with my head away from the window.

(Jan. 25, 1915)

We know now that fresh air did absolutely nothing to weaken the tuberculosis bacteria in the lungs. Clear, unpolluted air may have aided those patients to survive who had lived in highly polluted cities. Unfortunately, it probably made no difference for Fianna. Where she came from, the air was unpolluted even though it wasn't fresh mountain air.

The White Haven regimen of eggs and milk was essential, according to Dr. Flick. He wrote:

As the digestive organs and all those parts of the body which have to do with nutrition have been

[30]   Lawrence F. Flick, "Tuberculosis" Book V, Part 1 in *Household Companion: The Family Doctor,* ed. Johnson, Hill and Hartshorne. M. L Dewsnap, 1909. Library of Congress. https://archive.org (accessed 10/15/19).

weakened by the disease it is important to select food which is easily digested and assimilated. The best food for the treatment of tuberculosis is milk and the next best eggs. A good plan is to take three quarts of milk and six raw eggs a day and one meal of solid food.[31]

Today we know that an unbalanced diet this heavy with milk and eggs does not help in the body's struggle with tuberculosis. It can even be harmful because it places undue strain on a vulnerable system.

Fianna wrote a lot about food in her letters to her family. She wrote about how hard it was to force herself to drink all the milk and raw eggs she was supposed to imbibe and how sick this diet made her. She had terrible diarrhea and vomiting with severe stomach pain all through December.

After Samuel's interventions at Christmas, she wrote to Mary that she was "getting fine attention since Samuel was here" but that "my bowels have been so miserable again and then my stomach gets so sick." At this point, her letter writing was interrupted by a visit from Dr. Landis:

Dr. Landis was just now here and he made me so happy that I thought I must write right away. He saw how bad my bowels are and I said "I feel so sick in my stomach." He asked how much milk I take. I said I am to take 10 glasses of milk and 4 eggs but I only take 8—4. He said cut that down to six glasses of milk and three eggs. He said "now don't take anymore. We

---

[31] Ibid.

want to get your stomach into shape. It's the milk that makes you sick." I asked if I daren't have anything to eat then. He asked "if I get hungry." I said "yes." He asked if I don't get anything. I said nothing but fruit and I daren't eat that on account of my bowels. He told them to give me a light breakfast. I hope it will mean supper too. This is just what I was wanting. I am sure I can do better on taking nourishment that agrees with me than to force myself to something that doesn't.

(early Jan. 1915)

How grateful Fianna was for these changes! It was certainly helpful to be "taking nourishment" that would not make her sick.

In January, Fianna's letters began to include a small chart of her egg and milk intake, how often her bowels moved, and what her temperature was. Letters written at the end of the month list only 3 glasses of milk and 1 egg per day. Her digestive system seemed to have calmed down, but her temperature never got below 100°. She was feeling better even though she wasn't actually getting well. She wrote to Mary:

Do you see how nicely my bowels are doing since my stomach is getting used to meals again? I guess I don't need to tell you how much better I feel. I take one egg for the 9 o'clock diet and milk. I feel happy over it. I am glad the Doctors saw the remedy. It is a consolation to be cared for by the best Drs. in the state. They can do their part but the rest we must give into the hands of the Lord.

(Jan. 18, 1915)

The sheer relief of not being sick in her stomach and the gratitude she felt at being really listened to by the doctors helped Fianna endure the long days.

Fianna's letters frequently described the food she had for the big noon meal:

We had a very good dinner. Soup, bread & butter, mashed potatoes, stewed cauliflower, young chicken and some kind of pudding. The chicken was very young and tender.

(early Jan. 1915)

While diet was understood to be an essential part of her treatment, I think Fianna also wrote about food because not much was happening outside of mealtime. Dinner was the highlight of the day, matched only by letters from home!

She also wrote to Mary about foods she longed for:

If it isn't too much trouble I wish you could bring some cocoa along . . . And I am hungry for some of that strawberry preserves we made last spring . . . My appetite is very good and I want to satisfy it. I had fried potatoes and they were cold and souse and butter bread for supper . . . I ate butter bread and drank cold water and I thought about the jelly we made. They had tea but that makes me feel bad and you know what an old woman I am for something hot to drink. I am just glad I am feeling so well. I ate nearly all the souse and I never liked it. Ha![32]

(Jan. 28, 1915)

---

[32] Souse is usually made from pig's head, cooked and pickled in brine.

The third part of Dr. Flick's recipe for treatment of tuberculosis was rest. He advised that "during the fever stage of this disease absolute rest in bed is really necessary," although he acknowledged that moderate exercise when a patient was recovering could be "serviceable to recovery." Patients at White Haven had nothing to do but rest. They could read or write letters or visit with each other, but that's all there was to do.

When Fianna was particularly ill, she stayed in bed all the time. It was a very quiet life:

It is damp and rainy today but it feels good in bed. This is certainly a lazy life but that is what helps to cure tuberculosis.
Good-bye with love,
Fianna

(Jan. 25, 1915)

CHAPTER 16

LIVING A LIFE OF FAITH
AT THE SANATORIUM

Shaped by the church communities within which she had grown up, Fianna's Christian faith was the unquestioned center to her life, as solid within her as her bones, as natural to her as breathing. Fianna and Samuel believed in the power of prayer to heal. They looked to medicine for healing, but they also believed in a compassionate and powerful God. And they didn't hesitate to ask others for prayers, as this letter to her home congregation shows:

To the Members of the Little Swatara Church:-

After obeying the commandment of anointing according to James, I now ask the prayer of the whole church that I may regain my lost health and grow stronger in body and spirit.

When Peter was in prison the Church assembled and prayed so earnestly to the Heavenly Father that God send His holy angels at midnight to open the prison doors. That same God is our God and according to His sacred Word whatsoever we shall ask in His name believing that He will do.

(Jan. 12, 1915)

Fianna was asking the assembled church community to pray for her, just as the early church did for Peter. Samuel's letter described how the church received Fianna's request:

My dear Fianna:-

I was glad for your letter Saturday . . . It was touchingly given by Bro. Wenger. He could hardly read it and I guess he tried to make an impression. There were many who could not keep back the tears.

I guess it was a specimen of such rare spirituality that it was an eye opener to many who have too much sham religion.

(Jan. 18, 1915)

I can picture the plainly-dressed Brethren men and women gathered for their worship services in the old meeting-house with its white-plastered walls, wooden benches, and a simple pulpit table in the front where the bearded ministers, all dressed in black, sat together. Bro. Wenger announced he had a special request to bring before them. And, as he read the letter, his voice broke, and he could barely go on. Bro. Wenger was my great-grandfather, and I have heard him described as strict and stern. But this letter touched him deeply, and it touched the worshippers who had come to know and love Fianna. Their prayers were deep and heartfelt. There was no place for "sham religion" here!

In the letter below that Samuel wrote to brother Rufus and the rest of the Buchers, I learned that he believed the congregational prayer had helped Fianna:

Rufus, Naomi and family:-

... Somehow I feel that that was just the thing to do and that that was just the time to do it. It helped Fianna to keep up courage during that hardest spell she had since she left home. Her letters last week and this week show that she feels decidedly better. I remember last spring right after anointing she improved much.

If we pay an imaginary trip to Europe and think of the families broken up, of homes, houses, farms and churches ruined by a bitter and merciless war then we can begin but never finish to count our blessings ...

Two weeks ago when those letters from Fianna came that she had such a time & spell, I slept until a little after midnight and then my sleeping was done. When you have a good companion and know that she is not well and not even properly cared for that grinds.

I guess God has a purpose in view in giving us these experiences. I know that when Fianna is restored she will be nearer and dearer than ever.

Samuel

(Jan. 31, 1915)

This "hardest spell" that Samuel wrote about was described as an inflammation of the appendix by the White Haven doctors. Fianna endured great pain and remained in bed with an ice pack on her side. She recovered after a week and did not need an operation. Samuel was far away, however, and helpless in the face of it.

Samuel also referred to the "bitter and merciless war." Although the family letters focused on Fianna and small daily events, the writers were fully aware of the European war raging far away. Though the United States didn't enter World War I until 1917, the newspapers were filled with news from Europe. Samuel read and grieved the destruction and death, the separation of families, the lives ruined by the war. His own tragedy, his separation from loved ones and his fear of losing Fianna, did not close his heart to the suffering of others far away. I wonder if I could be so large-hearted.

Sister Mary wrote that the Mechanic Grove congregation, the church community that had watched Fianna grow up, prayed for her, too. "The Brethren lifted you up in prayer behind the pulpit tonight. I don't know how many asked about you today." And then, in typical Mary fashion, she turned to an account of little Leah's activities:

> Leah was naughty tonight in church. She wanted Teddy and I did not have him, and she cried. I took her in the cellar and picked up a corn cob and fixed my handkerchief on it for a shawl. Then it was alright . . .
> Sister Mary
>
> (Feb. 8, 1915)

While Fianna's religious communities and family were praying for her healing, she herself found opportunities at White Haven to live her faith. She didn't need to preach it in words; she simply lived it. She wrote Mary about the time her roommate "stole" some toast for her, and the spiritual quandary that created:

There are so many chances to let your light shine in a place like this. Yesterday morning while taking my milk I said to my room-mate "I wish I had a piece of toast to eat with this." Before I knew it she went out in the kitchen and stole two pieces of toast with butter and brought it to me. Well, I didn't know what to do. My conscience told me it was wrong to eat it as she had stolen it and I knew I would offend her by not taking it. After a while I said "I couldn't do it." She asked why. I said my conscience won't let me. She started to scold me, called me a foolish thing, etc. I left her talk but resolved in my heart not to take it. After she had cooled down I said "Maybe the Lord will let me get well on my conscience and if I don't have so much in my stomach." After a while she said "Of course it's stealing." I don't think she will do the favor again but she is very nice to me and respects me more than ever. It was a little thing but I am sure that toast would have been very hard to digest had I taken it.

(Jan. 6, 1915)

Fianna's cheerful faithfulness was tested again and again. In another letter to Mary, she wrote about the unfriendliness of some of the other patients. They were jealous because she received three meals a day, and they didn't:

I would have a lot to talk if you were here but I will tell you a few things that amuse me and sometimes provoke me. You know Mrs. Summers my roommate was very kind to me at first but after a while she got very bossy. She and the colored woman that is nearly always hanging around in our room around meal time are just like sisters. Well, they were my best friends at first and I felt very happy with them. They talked mean about every patient on the floor and since I get three meals and get such good attention they are so jealous of me that they hardly know what to do. I know that they talk mean about me. Mrs. S. asked her chief for three meals but he didn't order it for her and I got it without asking. The nurses give her breakfast and supper sometimes when there is enough just by their own good will. When it so happens that she gets nothing when I get supper, she sits down like a cross dog. She doesn't growl but won't talk and sometimes watches me the whole time. We had a splendid supper on Sat. evening and she didn't get any. She certainly was cross and cast up to me that they piled up our plates and gave us too much so she wouldn't have any. Now you can imagine how pleasant it is to eat under such conditions . . .

I just kept quiet and finished my supper and walked out and visited some patients at the other end of the hall that she doesn't like. I got too full and went over there to let it out . . . Ask Phares how he would enjoy studying Russia in this way. In a way I enjoy it because it is so babyish to be jealous. I just let them have their way. Just so I have the Lord with me to strengthen and help me.

(Jan. 18, 1915)

These stories tell me a lot about Fianna. She had the inner strength to bear illness and the long separation from her family and familiar community, but she also had the strength for the hard challenge of institutional living. She had no one to pray or read the Bible with her. It surely increased her loneliness that none of her neighbors in Rose Cottage cared about these things.

Her roommates talked "mean," and acted mean, too. I can understand Mrs. Sommers' jealousy. She wanted to be on Fianna's diet, too, and receive full dinners instead of milk, eggs and a bit of fruit. Her doctor didn't order it. And so she got angry with Fianna and acted like a "cross dog" watching Fianna eat.

Fianna's quiet, mild ways may have made her easy to "boss" around, but her roommate didn't understand the steadiness and strength that grounded Fianna. Even as the unpleasantness increased, she was determined to speak and act in keeping with Jesus' ways. She wrote to her family about hardships, but she didn't complain to the staff.

I wonder if some of the "meanness" that Fianna experienced was because she was different. Her dress was different, and she didn't join with the others in criticizing the staff or talking about other patients. It was not easy to live out the teachings of Christ in this setting. Though her body was not healing, her spirit was still strong. She was faithful to the ways she had been taught, and she witnessed to her Christian faith in this strange White Haven world:

The nurse brought my supper and said "There is no cocoa, just tea." I said "All right." She said "I never saw anybody like you. You are always satisfied with anything you get." I took it as a compliment.

(Jan. 28, 1915)

CHAPTER 17

LETTERS AND VISITORS

Fianna's spirit was strengthened through precious family visits and letters. While a visit was expensive and took one long day's travel, letters were daily events. By January, Samuel had even created a system for sending letters. He wrote to Mary:

> *What do you think of organizing to visit her daily? I visit her Tuesday and Friday of each week (by letter). If you can enlist anyone besides yourself to take one day a week <u>regularly</u> I would be glad. The thing I am aiming at is this. I would like to have definite understanding as to the time of mailing our letters so that Fianna gets one letter <u>every day</u> from the home folks . . . The letters must not necessarily be written on those days they can be written any time but could be mailed regularly so that no day passes by without paying Fianna a visit by letter from the home folks. Am I understood? Do you approve of it?*
>
> *Yours, Samuel*
>
> *Kiss baby Leah for me. I would like to see her.*
>
> (Jan. 26, 1915)

Mary wrote to Fianna that she thought the letter rotation would work well. But, she added, the family got confused the first week and that's why Fianna received no letters one day and three on another!

In early January, Fianna sent a postcard to Samuel's grandmother Gibbel with a picture of Rose Cottage on it. She wrote:

Dear Grandmother:-

This is a beautiful place and I like it very well. I am willing to do anything if it is the Lord's will for me to get well. Father and Mother were here yesterday. I long to see you. Can't you write me a letter? I would write a long letter but I must keep quiet in bed to get my fever down. My bed is on the porch. I take 8 glasses of milk and 4 raw eggs a day.

Fianna

(Jan. 4, 1915)

Rose Cottage, White Haven Sanatorium, postcard to Grandmother Gibbel

Fianna especially cherished Samuel's grandparents since hers had died before she was born. And Grandmother had lost her husband a few months earlier. That was surely in Fianna's mind as she wrote. Fianna's request for a letter from Grandmother Gibbel bore fruit. She wrote to her parents that she had received "a good letter from Grandmother Gibbel yesterday," and added, "I wish there were more like her."

Occasionally packages arrived and were very eagerly welcomed. In the beginning, Fianna received needed supplies, a comforter, bed socks, and caps to keep her warm. Later she asked for and received food parcels that included cocoa, pretzels, and Postum. And, in a letter to her mother, she asked for "those little kind of cakes you know."

She even received a chicken! She wrote to her mother of the unexpectedness of this package:

> . . . I am not so much in need of chicken. Hannah [Samuel's housekeeper] sent one. It slipped through somehow. The nurse asked me if it is something to eat. I said no. I was sure they wouldn't send anything. I was surprised it was then and I didn't want to tell her afterwards. It would have made a fuss and I didn't mean to tell a lie.
>
> Maybe I will confess after it is all. [finished]
>
> (Jan. 22, 1915)

I wonder if Fianna confessed after she and her friends enjoyed the chicken.

One very special package contained, not supplies for Fianna, but a beautiful dress that sister Mary made for little Leah.

In several of Mary's letters, she described this dress, the special tucks and flourishes, the silk embroidery thread, the challenge of setting the sleeves, and how their mother would make the buttonholes. But before little Leah wore it, Mary wanted Fianna to see it. She wanted to share her own delight in having created something so beautiful, and she knew it would give Fianna great pleasure to see it and imagine it on her daughter. Mary wrote:

Jan. 6. Hallelujah 'tis done, the dress is done. The dress and the letter start off together in the morning . . . You need not be in such a hurry to send it back. Am half ashamed to put it on her anyhow. I had no idea it would look so rich after it is finished.

(Jan. 6, 1915)

After Fianna received the package, she wrote to her sister:

Last evening I lay awake for a while. I felt overjoyed over Dolly's dress. There were three patients and a nurse in the room when I opened it. You should have heard all the expressions of delight. I took it to some of the other patients and they all thought it was so pretty. For my part I think it is most beautifully neat. I have it in my drawer and often take a peep at it. You certainly put a lot of work on it. The embroidery silk certainly makes it look rich and the goods made up so dainty. But now don't be foolish about putting it on her.

(early January 1915)

I wish *I* could see that dress! I understand Mary's hesitation to put little Dolly into a "rich" dress. Mary's world was one of hard work and plain living. Children could be dressed up nicely in bright colors but *too* much rich fabric and decoration was not in keeping with Brethren practice. It was prideful, as if one thought oneself better than others. The Brethren of southern Lancaster County where Mary lived were farmers. Mary wrote that she thought of having little Dolly wear it when they traveled to Elizabethtown for a meeting. Perhaps people there in the college town would appreciate it better.

Letters were good, packages were better, but visitors were the biggest highlight of these months. Samuel and Ammon came several more times, and members of Fianna's family found their way to White Haven, too.

The first to come after Christmas were her parents. While Fianna's parents had traveled widely in the Brethren ministry, this was a different journey, one of buggy, trolley, and train, followed by a sleigh ride up the mountain to the Sanatorium. Fianna wrote to Mary about her joy in this visit:

I certainly enjoyed parents' visit. The head nurse saw to it that they got some coffee. They don't all get that. She said to me that she thinks "they are such a nice old couple." Miss Cromsick (our nurse) went along out with them and helped them on the sleigh.

(Jan. 6, 1915)

In another letter to Mary, Fianna referred to gifts that their mother had brought along with her, gifts to share with the other patients:

Tell mother that young Polish girl that was in our room
likes her caps so well. She said it a couple of times. She asked me
if father could write. My room-mate said she knew he was an
intelligent man as soon as he opened his mouth.

(undated)

This visit was precious for Fianna. Her mother undoubt-
edly brought gifts of food with her as well as caps to share with
her roommates, probably knitted by herself or other churchwomen. Her parents' humble and kindly manner, as well as their
plain dress, brought respect from the staff and other patients.

I can picture Fianna's father going to other patients
and greeting them, asking their names and where their home
was. He was a man of presence, even in a tuberculosis sanatorium visiting his dying daughter. I was touched by the young
Polish girl's question, "Can he write?" Yes, he could read and
write. His formal schooling had ended after eight years, but
he continued to study and learn for the rest of his life. He had
even studied Greek to gain a deeper understanding of the New
Testament!

Fianna had other visitors. Her brother Rufus came, com-
bining a preaching commitment with a visit to his sister. And
there was the longed-for visit from little Dolly and sister Mary
who came with Fianna's youngest brother William. Mary's husband Phares, remaining at home, missed his opportunity to
learn more about Russia.

Fianna later sent a card to Mary with a picture of the
White Haven entrance, stone pillars framing the driveway that
led up the mountain. She wrote below the picture, "Do you

Entrance to White Haven Sanatorium, postcard to sister Mary

remember this place? I remember how I felt when I saw Dolly coming up the hill."

How eagerly Fianna awaited this visit and how overjoyed she was to see her little girl walk into the building! I hope they stayed for a long time, long enough for Dolly to get comfortable in the room and run around—and even get into mischief. Fianna hadn't seen her for several months, and she had grown in those months. Her vocabulary exploded with new words. I imagine Fianna couldn't take her eyes away from her as she explored this new place. It probably was hard for her to attend to William and Mary's conversation. I think she walked with her daughter to other rooms and introduced little Dolly to the patients there. Saying goodbye was the painful part. I picture Fianna walking to the door of Rose Cottage to watch them climb into the sleigh.

This visit was around the time of Leah's second birthday on January 20th. Fianna sent her daughter a birthday postcard:

To my little Dolly with wishes and prayers that she may see many more happy birthdays and that she may live to be a good little woman.

from your Loving Mamma

Fianna's wish for her daughter's future came true. She lived to be "a good little woman" and a wonderful aunt for my brother and me.

CHAPTER 18

SAMUEL'S HARDEST VISIT

By early February, Fianna had acute abdominal pain again. Since it was primarily in her side, the physicians suspected appendicitis. They treated her with ice packs and complete bed rest. Surgery for appendicitis was fairly new in 1915. If Fianna needed an operation, she would have to leave White Haven and enter a city hospital. Writing to Mary, she admitted that she felt discouraged and homesick:

My dear Sister:-

I have been real sick since you are here. Could hardly walk and last evening Dr. ordered me to stay in bed. It certainly feels best here. The nurses are very kind to me . . . The Dr. thoroughly examined me last night. It isn't in the region of the appendix but he thought it might turn into peritonitis.

I wished for home this week but I have picked up courage again. I didn't get mother's cakes quite all [finished] and now I can't eat them. I have cold all around. My temperature tells that. Now I do wish mother wouldn't worry. I am getting better . . .

much love,

Fianna

(Feb. 4, 1915)

Fianna's pain didn't come from peritonitis, an infection in the abdomen that would have killed her quickly. Although it may have been appendicitis, the symptoms diminished over the next week. It was the worst pain she'd had since her initial trouble with the milk and eggs diet, and being so far from home made it even harder. Her courage flagged, but she picked it up again. I am awed by the indomitable strength of this grandmother I never knew.

Fianna was caught between wishing for her mother's presence and not wanting her mother to worry about her. In the letter below, she tried to write cheerfully about her situation, but she was honest about longing for a motherly presence in the midst of her pain:

Dear Father & Mother:-

I am happy that I have good news to tell you. Dr. Armstrong saw me again last evening. After he examined me he said "you are getting along all right. You don't need to have an operation." The Dr. here comes to see me morning and evening . . . My side is still very painful and tender . . . They still keep ice on. The nurses are very kind to me but I did wish to be with mother during this spell. I thank God it is getting all right . . .

(early February 1915)

A week later, Mary wrote to her sister:

We all think of you so much especially if we know you are not well. Am so glad Samuel is with you.

When mother found out this morning that you are not well

and Samuel is going out, she said she was going, too. We told her
then to wait and see what Samuel has to say after he gets there . . .
(Feb. 11, 1915)

Yes, the home folks *were* worried for her. Fianna's mother,
who under normal conditions would only travel with her husband, was desperate enough to declare she was going to White
Haven when Samuel did. She needed to be there, to be with
her daughter. I would have wanted to fly to Fianna's side, too—
and stay there! But Mary persuaded her to wait.

Samuel's visit to Fianna at White Haven was his hardest visit. He traveled without Ammon this time. From White
Haven, he wrote unexpected news to her family. Fianna was to
come home:

My dear Phares, Mary & all:-
  . . . I was in town this morning to see Dr. Armstrong
again. He is giving his attention to Fianna regularly . . .
  Dr. Armstrong recommends that we take Fianna home so
that if another attack on the appendix occurs then we would be
nearer to the hospital for an operation. There is no immediate
danger. They have checked the attack and Dr. Armstrong thinks
that in about a week she might be able to be moved on a cot. She
is to go on a cot so that there will be no danger of pus form-
ing. She will there also get better attention and better meals than
here . . .
  I would have liked to stay here on the reclining chair and
wait on Fianna day and night but that is contrary to the rules
to stay at night.

I also expect to see Dr. Weiss from Leb. [Lebanon] on Sat. when I return. I want him to attend to Fianna at home. He is a hospital Dr. Dr. Kerr shall never come under our roof again (for professional work) if I can avoid it.

Samuel

(Feb. 12, 1915)

The Dr. Kerr whom Samuel banished had attended to Baby Rufus when he was dying, and probably attended Fianna also. He had misdiagnosed her, treating her for stomach troubles, not tuberculosis. Dr. Weiss, on the other hand, was a hospital physician who had studied widely and was well respected. He had recommended White Haven, and Samuel trusted him.[33]

Samuel stayed two nights at White Haven before returning home and traveling with Ammon to a Bucher family gathering. It was a rare opportunity for Ammon and his sister Leah to be together again. In a postcard to her mother, Fianna wrote:

I am thinking of my dear family being with you all today. I wonder what the children did when they saw each other. I am feeling much better. The pain in my side is about gone. I can eat better too. I shall be glad when I can eat at home. I have learned a lot here and I think I can do just as well at home. But I hate to miss the mountain air . . .

Fianna

(Feb. 15, 1915)

---

[33] Dr. Weiss' obituary states that "his name was a household one and his reputation extended far beyond the confines of the county." *Lebanon Daily News,* June 18, 1915, p. 11.

I, too, wonder what the children did when they saw each other. Did little Leah remember Ammon? Postcards had been flowing between the children while they were apart. I can picture Aunt Mary exclaiming, "Look, Dolly, you have another postcard from your brother Ammon. See how pretty it is." Dolly knew that someone named Ammon was important. Ammon liked receiving mail, too. Even when the note from "your sister Leah" was actually from Aunt Mary with news for Samuel, he saved the card in his postcard book.

But Samuel couldn't rejoice in his children being once more together. He came home with a very heavy heart. He was carrying the worst of news, so painful that he didn't write it in the letter sent to Mary and Phares. He probably shared it with Fianna's family when he was with them. Later, after Fianna's death, he wrote a long letter to Fianna's older sister Annie Bucher King[34] and told of his anguish:

Feb. 12 I will never forget for it was then that I was told in plain straightforward word, that Fianna cannot live. I was not to tell her and had nobody else I could tell it to. I stayed with her all that day and in spite of her condition I was not allowed to stay with her that night. I lodged (wept and prayed) in the valley that lies between White Haven and White Haven Sanatorium. Fianna was over on the hill, Ammon was at home this

---

[34] After Fianna's death, both Samuel and sister Leah wrote very long letters to Annie Bucher King, who lived in Virginia, telling the story of Fianna's last months. The letters circulated among the family, and copies were saved by Samuel for his children.

time, Baby Leah was with Aunt Mary, Rufus was in Heaven, and I was alone with that sad news heavy on my heart and no-body to tell it to but I could wept and pray over it all.

(April 29 and May 2, 1915)

What a painful gathering for the family when Samuel told them. Tears and a stunned grief replaced the joy of see-ing the children together. Samuel stayed overnight with the Buchers, and they laid plans to bring Fianna home. Brother William and sister Mary would travel to White Haven with Samuel the following weekend. If she were strong enough, they would bring her home then. It would be a bumpy ride down the mountain, a long rail trip to Lebanon, and then the buggy ride home. Fianna was to travel on a cot in the luggage car with her dear ones seated by her. Her parents and Ammon would wait for her at home.

A letter Samuel wrote two days before Fianna came home shows how tenaciously he clung to hope. He *couldn't* give her up!

My dear Phares, Mary & family:-

I have a letter from Fianna today that sounds better. She is on her feet again. Her pain is gone in the region of her appendix. I am trying to hope that those Drs. are liars. Drs. are. If it is God's will that she shall be spared any way no matter what Dr. say. Perhaps it was to come so far so that we can see the finger of God in her recovery.

(Feb. 18, 1915)

And Fianna, not knowing what the lying doctors had foretold, wrote quite cheerfully to her parents just before she returned home:

Dear father and mother:-

... I guess this is the last letter I shall write at White Haven. I am anxious to go home since I know it is for the better. I will have better care at home and will have a good Doctor too. I hope Hannah can keep up with it ...

... If I could buy my lost health that is the first thing I would do. I am glad Samuel and the children are so well ...

Lovingly,

      Fianna

                    (Feb. 19, 1915)

CHAPTER 19

"I Am Going Home"

FREDERICKSBURG WOMAN BROUGHT HOME ON COT was a headline in the hometown newspaper as Fianna came home. The article gave further details:

> Mrs. Meyers who is a tubercular patient, was unable to stand on her feet, she was placed on a cot and made the journey to this city from Allentown in that position. The cot was placed in the baggage car of the noon express and arrived in this city at 1:05 this afternoon. She was accompanied to this city by her husband, S.G. Meyers, a well-known resident of Fredericksburg, and several friends . . . Her appearance stretched out on a cot, attracted considerable attention at the station and much sympathy for her condition was expressed by her fellow passengers on the train and in many passengers awaiting trains at the depot.[35]

Once she arrived home, Fianna was immediately put to bed. The journey had been an exhausting one, but there was such comfort to be at home again, surrounded by the familiar and the well loved. She saw it all eagerly. Ammon was

---

[35] I have been unable to document the source of this clipping.

there! And her mother! I can imagine the hugs and the tears. She had been gone two and a half months. She was returning home, not cured, as she had hoped, but in worse health. But she did return home to her family. For Samuel and the rest of the family, their gladness at having her home covered the deep, secret grief they shared. Fianna was not expected to live.

Although Fianna's mother had seen her in early January, seeing her now was heartbreaking. In January she could walk, but now she was bedfast. Her mother had learned that the doctors expected Fianna to die. She would lose her youngest daughter, the one who carried her name. I have no letters written by Fianna's mother, and I don't know how she endured this. I believe her faith in God's will gave her courage and comfort, as it did for the others who loved Fianna.

Over the next few days, Fianna's parents and siblings, Mary and William, returned to their homes. But Fianna's sister Leah came to be with Fianna and her family. She planned to remain a week until their mother could come again. She stayed on, however, leaving her job as a housekeeper for two months until after her sister's death.

Like Samuel, Leah also wrote a long letter to her sister Annie in Virginia, telling her the story of those weeks with Fianna. In this letter, Leah described how she felt when Fianna came home:

I had not given her up as a hopeless case. I could not, even after the doctors said she could not live. I trusted in a higher power and I thought it could not be. The first time Dr. Weiss was to see her after I was there, he told me, "There is nothing to

be done but to try to make her comfortable while she is here, then
you have nothing to regret after she is gone." I told him I cannot
give her up as long as there is life, I will hope.

On Thursday night she was anointed. She told the Brethren,
"It is my desire to get well, but I am submissive to His will." It came
again as a shock to me for I was not ready to say, "Thy will be done."

On Saturday I unpacked her trunk put her clothes
away. I said to her, "I guess when you get up you have to hunt
for your things." She said, "Yes, if I can hunt." I said nothing
but worked hard to keep back the tears. Mother was coming
next week when I was leaving. So I said, "When mother leaves,
I am coming again." She said, "You are kind."

The night before I was going to leave she had such a weak
spell, then I decided to stay, but did not tell her until the next
morning. She was so glad. As long as my life shall last I shall
never regret that I stayed.

(May 7, 1915)

Fianna's bed was set up in "the front room," and Samuel
slept in the room next to it. Leah wrote that he "watched while
he slept," going to her as soon as she stirred. In the morning
he still had to go to the bank. Hannah managed the housework. Leah helped, too, but most of her attention went to her
sister—and to her beloved little nephew Ammon. The nursing
care for her sister included feeding her, cleaning up when she
vomited, bathing and changing her, and, most of all, keeping
her company. Fianna, weakening daily, remained in bed.

One of Leah's regular tasks was writing to her parents,
telling them how Fianna was doing. There was little good news:

Dear Mother:-

I suppose you are looking for something from us today.
Fianna rested better last night than she did since she came home.
. . . She took an egg in milk last evening and then she had to vom-
it. She still has a good bit of pain in her stomach but not any at
her appendix. Br. Jacob Pfautz and a Bro. Eshelman have been
here this forenoon. Bro. Eshelman is from Elizabethtown and is
preaching at the Union House just now. Samuel's mother is com-
ing . . .

          Leah

          (Feb. 25, 1915)

In the envelope for this letter, I found a piece of paper covered with pencil scribbles. On it was written "To Grandma from
Ammon." I can picture three-year-old Ammon, full of energy
and questions, wanting to know what his Aunt Leah was doing
when she sat down to write to her mother. Then *he* wanted to
write to Grandma, too. Leah, like a good aunt, gave him pencil
and paper, and he scribbled a few lines. He watched as she carefully folded and inscribed it, then placed it in the envelope with
her letter. Thus it was preserved for the next century.

In another letter, Leah wrote about flowers that someone
brought to Fianna and the pleasure they gave her:

Dear Phares and Mary:-

The flowers came yesterday a little wilted but after they have
been in water for a little bit they stood up nicely and are now
beautiful and are filling their mission. Fianna often says, "O, you
pretty flowers." She wondered if the children send the daisies be-

So many visitors tired her even when she was glad to see them.

Sometimes Fianna's visitors did not know how to visit. Some stayed too long or were too loud or simply insensitive. In one letter to sister Mary, Samuel mentions someone who wanted to visit. Since this person lived at a distance, he thought they should ask her to stay overnight. But they reconsidered:

"Leah and Fianna talked about it and they thought it was only wearing on Fianna if some one strange is there . . . perhaps you would better discourage that idea."

(March 18, 1915)

In the same letter to Mary, Samuel wrote of how he felt as he watched Fianna weakening:

Her stomach is upset again. I am afraid it will leave her weaker. She did not rest well until after 2 o'clock last night.

Dr. Weiss is hopeless about her. He was there Sunday and said she will likely just waste away and wear out. He said further that she might (<u>but not likely will</u>) have a hemorrhage or clot of blood pass into circulation from a bowel tubercle (?). I am hoping for the best and at the same time getting ready for anything else.

If it is the Lord's will, we believe that she can still be restored to full health and if it is not we will have to be reconciled to that.

I am enclosing a check that you can use as you see fit.[36]

---

[36] Samuel's check helped to pay for his daughter's needs.

. . Ammon is picking up some german expressions. He heard some one say the other day, "Is der Samuel um der wake?"[37] and then he repeated it so funny.

I want you to kiss baby Leah for me.

Samuel

(March 18, 1915)

Dr. Weiss was "hopeless," meaning that he had no hope for Fianna's recovery. Dr. Weiss was preparing Samuel and the rest of Fianna's family for her death. Samuel tried to be reconciled to it and, at the same time, he believed that God could do a miracle. It is hard to imagine how he continued going to the bank every day, but he did. He knew Fianna was well cared for by her sister.

In spite of his pain, he was still Samuel, and he still had a sense of humor. A week later he wrote to Mary about her upcoming visit and his own sense that the end was coming:

Dear Phares, Mary & All:-

We received your card yesterday. You ask whether you are to bring baby Leah along. Well it is a question in my mind whether I will take you out from Lebanon if you come without her. Now you know and Fianna also said she wants her to come. Come this week sure.

Fianna is dropping lower week by week. There are days when she seems a little brighter and then worse again. So all told she is going and she knows she is getting weaker.

---

[37] In Pennsylvania German, Ammon said, "Is Samuel around?"

... She said last night that she wants to suffer God's will. I said I don't know why this must all be. Then she said she thinks her time is up.

They tell me that clouds have a silver lining and that that side of this heavy cloud is turned away from us now. Perhaps we will some day see it clearly and understand.

If I had to live life over I would surely marry the same sweet heart. I would try to show her more kindnesses. Our union was the result of much prayer and careful thinking and I feel and I know you all feel that it was not a mistake.

Don't think that you are making it inconvenient for me to fetch you. I am glad to do it and need the fresh air and the confidential talk.

Your brother,

S.G.M

(March 29, 1915)

I am glad that Fianna saw her little Dolly again. Mary and Phares probably stayed for several days. I can picture little Leah running into her mother's room and all around the room, climbing up on the chairs, perhaps onto the bed. Her mother would reach out and stroke her hair. Leah was two years old, and talked a lot. Did her antics and chatter bring smiles to Fianna's face? I imagine Mary trying to make the little girl sit quietly on her lap and "be good," but little Leah wriggled and wanted to get down so she could explore this house that was only faintly familiar to her. Probably she explored the outdoors, too, visiting the chickens and the other animals with her father and brother.

When it was time for Mary to return home, both she and Fianna knew it was the long goodbye. I wonder how they spoke together about it. They believed they would meet again in heaven, but this was still separation. Fianna knew that Mary would continue to care for little Leah as if she were her own, but she still had to let her go. Although she'd reached the place of "submission to God's will," this goodbye was wrenching.

Mary returned home, and sister Leah continued nursing Fianna and painfully writing regular bulletins:

Dear Mother & all:-

This is one of my hardest tasks. I have to write and don't know what to say. Fianna said I shall tell you she is glad when you folks are coming . . .

Fianna did not rest so well last night she had pain. She told me this morning she don't eat because she is hungry but just eats to get something in her stomach. She often says she feels weak.

Leah

I asked Ammon whose boy he is. He said "Papa's & Mamma's mucher, Aunt Leah's a little bit and Hannah's a little. That's all."

(March 30, 1915)

Writing to the home folks was hard for Leah. She included little snippets about Ammon to fill the page, but Fianna was slipping away and there was nothing more important to say. The physical care she gave her sister was easier than writing letters home.

When this letter was written, Fianna had less than two

weeks to live. She was weak and had more bouts of pain. Constant coughing exhausted her. Leah wrote, "She did not eat much but ate nearly an hour. Sometimes she fell asleep during this time."

In Samuel's long letter to sister Annie King written after Fianna's death, he recounted conversations he and Fianna had had when she knew she would not live:

> We did not tell her [she was dying] until she had given up completely all hope of recovery. We then had a chance to talk things over about the future. She was so glad I told her and she took so much interest in my and the children's future.
>
> (Apr. 29, 1915)

Leah described those last days in her long letter to sister Annie:

> . . . The last Friday night that she was with us, she was so weak . . . Samuel said, "he is not going to bed tonight, she talks delirious." We did not leave her alone. She coughed all night and slept very little . . . After dinner she had a weak spell that Hannah and I both thought she was dying. I phoned for Samuel to come home. He was there so soon I thought it could not be possible that he is here. When he came Hannah was washing her face and I was bathing her feet. We heard Samuel coming and she (Fianna) thought if we are doing this when he comes in he might be frightened. When he came in the room, she looked at him and smiled. Afterwards she said, "Maybe it was not necessary to raise such excitement."
>
> After he was home a little while she said to him, she is

wishing mother would be here. Samuel phoned to her and she said they intend coming tomorrow (Sunday). Samuel said, "Don't wait until tomorrow."

A little later she expressed herself to me by saying, "This won't last long anymore." She was just as calm and patient as she could be. About 7:00 father, mother, William and Rufus came in the machine. She heard them before I did. When I went to the window and saw them running slowly and turning in, I told her they are turning in, she brightened up and said, "Is it a relief to you too since they are here?" It surely was.

All of Saturday night until Sunday at 3:30 P.M. we were with her. "To watch the coming of her long pulseless sleep."[38] Peter, Samuel's brother Levi and [Levi's] wife (Annie Crouse) came at noon and were also there with her. They did not all stay in the room all the time. On Sunday she said once "I am glad mother is so brave." Annie, it was hard to be brave and bear up, but I am glad I could be with her. You know I never saw anyone die before this. It was hard to see it but Oh so beautiful to stand by the side of such a one as she was passing over the River of Death. As long as memory lasts we shall remember the beautiful words spoken . . . "I am going to my Beautiful heavenly Home," "I am so happy." I believe that she saw more than human eyes could see.

The Doctor was there Saturday evening about 10 o'clock . . . The next morning he came again. She told him she was disappointed this morning. She did not expect to be here anymore. He talked a little with her and left the room with tearful eyes. He had talked to me one time before about her cheerful

---

[38]   From "Thoughts of Heaven," author unknown.

spirit and that it is too bad there is nothing to be done for her. When he came downstairs Sunday morning mother told him, "her feet are cold." He said, "Yes, her hands are cold too." Oh! how cruel is the cold hand of Death! . . .

I truly believe that she would not have lasted as long as she did if it had not been for Samuel and the children. Possibly a week before she died, she said, "If I would allow myself, I could easily make it that it would be hard to leave this world, but I can easily leave everything but Samuel and the children." Often during her last hours when Samuel and I were sitting in front of the bed, she would say, "Papa, Papa, Papa," [referring to Samuel] and sometimes had hold of his hand. But the Lord called her and she had to go alone. Papa, whom she loved most dearly, was left behind. We trust to bring up his two little lambs in the Master's service.

We tried to make her comfortable but her pain we could not remove. She did not often say anything about it. She did bear her suffering patiently. She sometimes said she hopes Samuel and I will receive a blessing for what we are doing and that no one can fix her pillow as good as Samuel and I. It is a comfort to know this . . . The last we could do for her was to cover her cold body with the soft, white blanket until the resurrection morn. I am more homesick this week than I have ever been . . .

(May 7, 1915)

Someone sat by Fianna's bed and wrote down her last conversations in pencil. I'm holding the yellowed paper as I read the words:

Fianna: "Leah take me home."

Leah: "I would if I could but I can't. Each one has to go alone. Be patient it won't be long."

Fianna: "Do you think it won't?"

Leah: "No you are passing through the valley now. Jesus will come to take you."

Fianna: "Lord take me."

And another brief conversation with her brother William:

Fianna: "William, if I die do you think I will go to heaven?"

William: "Yes."

Fianna: "Do you surely think I will?"

William: "Yes, without a doubt."

Fianna: "William will you promise me to get ready?"

William: "Yes. Yes I will sometime."

And with Samuel:

Fianna: "I am going to my beautiful heavenly home."

Samuel: "We will also come sometime."

Fianna: "I will wait for you inside the gates."

And finally:

"Oh Lord take me to my heavenly home." Fianna said these words probably 100 times or more during all of Saturday night & Sunday.

Fianna died on Sunday afternoon, April 11, 1915. By her bedside were her parents, her sister Leah, her brothers William and Rufus, and her husband Samuel.

CHAPTER 20

THE COMMUNITY GATHERS

As was the custom among the Brethren of that time, Fianna's body remained at home in the parlor before the funeral. She was dressed in the same white dress she wore when she married. Funeral invitations state that it was to be held "at the residence." It was followed by a graveside service and then a public service in the Union Meeting House next to the cemetery where she was buried. Samuel's long letter to Fianna's sister Anna names the hymns used for all three services. They

Funeral announcement to friends and family

151

were followed by a dinner for everyone in the basement of the church. It was a long, exhausting day for all of the family.

The local Lebanon newspaper reported:

> The funeral of Mrs. Samuel G. Meyer was held from the late home on Saturday morning. Services were held in the Union Meeting House and interment was made in the cemetery adjoining. The remains rested in a gray cloth covered casket. Services were conducted by Rev. E. M. Wenger of this place, and Rev. Hartzler of Elizabethtown. They took for their text: Gen. 31: 49—The Lord watch between me and thee while we are absent one from another . . .
>
> This was one of the largest funerals held in this place for a long time. The meetinghouse was filled and many could not gain admission.
>
> The meal was served in the basement of the meetinghouse and overflowed . . .[39]

Another news article was more specific in reporting that 400 persons dined and 125 horses were fed at "one of the largest funerals ever held in this vicinity."[40] This was a huge gathering of church and community with many attendees traveling a distance to be present. The obituary in the *Quarryville Sun* even included information on how best to travel to the funeral:

> Those wishing to go will take the 5:30 am car in Quarryville, and in Lancaster the Reading train for Lebanon. They will be met by teams in Lebanon. Those wishing to go will please advise George Bucher, Quarryville.[41]

---

[39] *Lebanon Semi-Weekly News,* April 22, 1915, p. 3.

[40] *Lebanon Semi-Weekly News,* April 22, 1915, p. 7.

[41] *Quarryville Sun,* Tuesday, April 13, 1915, p. 5. To take the "car" from Quarryville is traveling by trolley into Lancaster.

When I was a child, my family occasionally attended worship services in the Union Meeting House. This plain white building is set at an intersection of country roads. Across the road is a one-room schoolhouse (now converted to a home) where my father and his siblings attended school and where Samuel and a couple of Samuel's brothers taught. The cemetery is on a third quadrant. Here the land rises gently upward and the view from the cemetery over the farmed or wooded fields extends as far as the misty blue mountains of the Appalachians. It is a beautiful and peaceful place.

I imagine this country corner as it may have been on Saturday, April 17, 1915. The nearby fields were clogged with buggies. Perhaps automobiles were parked in another field. There would have been a hitching rail, but I don't think it was long enough for all the horses that day. I wonder if there was an enclosed area for the horses or if they remained with the buggies.

The churchwomen had mobilized to provide food for the meal after the funeral. Big pots of soup or meat, a mountain of bread, many mounds of butter, rounds of cheese, and lots and lots of pies and cakes were carried into the church basement. The church people knew they would be feeding a host, and they knew how to manage large crowds. Church groups gathered together often for large denominational meetings with food provided by the hosting community.

People who came early were able to sit inside the building, but I imagine crowds of people standing outside on the small grassy area next to the road. Were the windows open so those standing outside could catch the sermon? Could they hear when the congregation sang "Nearer My God to Thee" or "Safe in the Arms of Jesus"? Did they join in the singing? Brethren congregations did not use musical instruments in worship, but they sang with great fervor.

The community that gathered came from all the chapters of Fianna's life—except the White Haven chapter. All family members who possibly could come were present. The Buchers (her father's family), the Pfautzs (her mother's family), the Wengers, the Meyers and the Gibbles (Samuel's families) were all large. Fianna and Samuel had many aunts, uncles, cousins, nieces, and nephews. They flocked in from all around south-central Pennsylvania and beyond.

Even beyond the host of relatives, attendees came from several strong Brethren communities where Fianna was well known. I wonder how many persons traveled from the Quarryville area by train. Since both her family and Samuel's family were leaders within church circles, persons might attend this funeral because they knew the families even if they didn't know Fianna. Perhaps they'd attended evangelistic services led by father George or brother Rufus or uncle Christian Bucher or uncle Edward Wenger. Perhaps they knew Fianna's oldest sister Mary and her husband I. N. H. Beahm who had served as Elizabethtown College's first president. The college community where she and Samuel had been students just a few years earlier would have been well represented. They knew her and Samuel well.

And there was the non-Brethren community. The local people knew Samuel and all his family. After all, they saw him regularly. He was the cashier in the local bank and handled their money. His father and grandfathers were community leaders, and the family had been settled in the area since colonial times. With deep roots such as this, everyone joined them during their time of sorrow.

In Samuel's long letter to sister Annie King, he wrote about the funeral service:

You likely know that I asked the brethren to use Laben's words as a text when he said, "The Lord watch between me and thee when we are absent one from another." They spoke on the following points.

1. *The Lord's watch (my greatest need)*
2. *A heartful of good intentions*
3. *Genuine love*
4. *Covenant making*
5. *Separation*
6. *Meeting again*
7. *Dispensations of Providence*

(April 29, 1915)

These "points" tell a great deal about the faith that strengthened Samuel and Fianna during their marriage and through their tragic early separation. Theirs was a genuine love and their marriage a covenant. Not only were the marriage promises made to each other but also to God *for* each other. And now, in their time of separation, there was another covenant. Love would continue, Fianna would wait for Samuel "inside the gates," and, even as Samuel continued living without his sweetheart, the "Lord's watch" would strengthen and uphold him.

CHAPTER 21

"Now the Worse
Is Yet to Come"

Fianna's life story came to an end, but the story of Fianna's family continued. Their stories are part of Fianna's story, too. Fianna's absence shaped their lives as surely as her presence would have done.

After the funeral, Samuel said to Leah, "Now the worse is yet to come." This is true for everyone who has experienced the death of one they loved. When the loved one has been a daily companion, the loss is profound. Reshaping life with an enormous hole at its center begins after the funeral is over, when the extended family and friends return to their own lives, and the grieving spouse is left alone. In a letter fragment I have, Samuel named some of what he would miss: "the sweet voice, the smile of cheer, the hand to press and the heart to love."

For a week after the funeral, Sister Leah remained with Samuel and Ammon. In the long letter to her sister Annie King, she wrote about Fianna's children:

The day after the funeral, we were in the room where she was lying when sick. I said to Baby Leah, "Where is Mam-

ma?" *She ran around the foot end of the bed, in front of the bed and looked all over the bed. She will not remember her, as she is so young. Ammon will. He still talks about baby Rufus . . .*

Ammon talks a good bit about her. Things like this, "Mamma's body is in the parlor." "Mamma went to Heaven." "Mamma is sleeping a long, long sleep." "Can't Mamma eat anymore?" "Can't you feed her anymore?" "Can Mamma walk now?" "Aunt Leah must get another Mamma for me." One day I polished his shoes. He said, "I want to show them to Papa. I can't show them to Mamma."

(May 7, 1915)

As I read little Ammon's words, I regretted again that I had never asked my father about his mother. What did he remember? What wispy memories were stored in his heart?

Leah helped to clean out the house after the funeral. She wrote to Annie about the precautions against infection they had taken in caring for Fianna, using only paper tissues and paper cups, and carefully burning them. She wrote about fumigating the rooms and hanging the clothes outdoors and that "A germ cannot live longer than two hours in the sunshine." She washed, ironed, and packed away her sister's clothing. I think practical, hard-working Leah found comfort in these physical tasks.

In Leah's letter to Annie, she also wrote about Fianna and Samuel's marriage:

I did not get in the home so often but when I did go I stayed a while. Never did I hear an unkind word spoken and he helped her so nicely with her work and the children. Nothing ever seemed too much trouble for him.

A day before she died, she said to me, "If there is an ideal home ours was one." And it truly was.

(May 7, 1915)

Samuel's grief poured out through letters he wrote to friends and family. In his letter to Annie, he wrote:

Annie, our union was the result of much prayer and careful thinking and I feel that it was no mistake. I would do the same things over only if I had more wisdom I would likely here and there drop in an extra kind word and deed. I have nothing particularly to regret but the loss so great . . .

What would I do without the children? The joy they bring and the responsibility they justly claim is equally great. They hold in store for me some of their Mamma's sunshine.

(Apr. 29, 1915)

In a letter to one of his brothers, Samuel wrote about the loss of both Baby Rufus and Fianna:

When the branch was broken from the tree it hurt but when the very trunk was split in two the wound is beyond repair in this life.

(Aug. 1, 1915)

How did my grandfather continue living with the split trunk that was a "wound beyond repair?" I found some clues.

He was comforted through the many letters he received. He wrote to his brother, "I got some letters last week and these do me a lot of good." And to Fianna's parents, he wrote, "I have many friends whom I thought were only acquaintances." Between family and church communities, he was surrounded with love, and he knew that he was held in prayer.

While Samuel's own family supported him, he also continued to be brother and son to the Buchers. Fianna had particularly desired this closeness for him. Leah wrote to her sister Annie King:

One of her last and great concerns was that after she is gone we not neglect or forsake Samuel, and the friendship that exists between us and him will always remain the same. I for one should be grieved double if I would know that our friendship would grow cold. We could not keep our Fianna but we are glad we have a Samuel and that he has a confiding trust in us.

(May 7, 1915)

Although I only have the letters Samuel wrote, not those he received, I know Fianna's family wrote him during this time. In October, Samuel wrote one letter with separate sections for each of the Bucher families who lived close to each other, thereby responding to all their individual letters at one time. To "mother and father," he wrote:

Thanks for the letter mailed some time ago and the card and the stockings . . . Thank God for such parents that raised such a daughter . . .

(Oct. 15, 1915)

In the section of this letter addressed to Mary and Phares, Samuel expressed more of his grief:

Thanks for the cards and the sunshine they brought into my life. This means so much since the sunshine is so scarce. As time carries us away from the hour of separation, things that Fianna did and words that she said become very sacred. If it were not for the dear little ones, I could easily wish my body hid in a grave and my soul in the sleeping chambers of paradise. But our God who can see both the sunshine and the shadows likely has a purpose in view in giving us a being in this world and putting us through all this schooling.

(Oct. 15, 1915)

He added a message for Baby Leah:

To Baby Leah - There are times when we are just a little home sick for you but we know you are well taken care of when Aunt Mary and Grandma have charge of you.

(Oct. 15, 1915)

While little Dolly continued living with Mary and Phares, Ammon remained with Samuel. Housekeeper Hannah cared for him during the day while Samuel was at the bank. But in the morning and evening, this little boy was Samuel's responsibility. Of course, having a three year old to care for complicated Samuel's mornings and evenings. In a letter written to Fianna's parents, he was interrupted several times by Ammon:

Ammon is here saying, "I am tired, I am tired." So I will take him to bed and finish tomorrow . . .

I guess you never got such a patched up letter. I had just started writing this morning when Ammon got out of bed and came half way down the stairway and called me. I dressed him . . .

(started May 2, completed May 6, 1915)

Having Ammon with him was a comfort for Samuel. Samuel was a giver, and, even in his great pain, caring for Ammon was good for him. Ammon needed his father. The story of their lives together unfolds through postcards sent from Ammon to his little sister, Leah. I imagine Ammon seated by his father, interrupting him as he was responding to letters he had received. I imagine his father suggesting that perhaps he'd like to send a postcard to his sister. And then Ammon told his father what to say:

Dear Sister:-

I am well. I eat much and sleep a lot. I wave good bye to Papa every morning. I used to wave from my chair at the breakfast table but now I go along with papa to the barn and kiss him and then wave when he is on the buggy.

Ammon

P.S. I will kiss papa for you.

(May 3, 1915)

Dear Sister:-

Papa thinks I am naughty sometimes. This week Hannah

Postcard from Ammon to his sister Leah, May, 1915

got an orange ready for me. It was a dry one. I said "Pusy [cat] may eat it." Hannah said she would eat it and did. Then I said to her, "Hannah you are a pusy."

Ammon

(May 23, 1915)

My dear Sister:-

Yesterday morning Papa went out in the field to cultivate corn about 4:a.m. When I got awake I was soon out to help him. I am a farmer boy. I feed the little pigs. I like papa & you. Hannah a little bit. Aunt Leah mucher.

Ammon

(June 2, 1915)

In spite of Samuel's efforts to keep the family bonds strong, the reality was that little Leah lived with Aunt Mary. Once Ammon said to his father, "When Mamma was well, she kept baby Leah for Aunt Mary." Samuel would have smiled at that innocent observation even while it hurt him. Little Leah had spent most of her life living with Mary and Phares, but her father Samuel loved her and wanted her to be his baby. His letters or postcards to Mary and Phares are filled with questions about her. "Has Baby Leah's fear of Collie not changed to love yet?" "Does she still find a basin of water when it is within sight and reach?" All his letters end with "Kiss baby Leah for me."

In one envelope, I found a check from the First National Bank of Fredericksburg where Samuel worked. Dated May 17, 1915, it "paid to the order of baby Leah one thousand kisses" and was signed "Papa."

In a letter to Mary and Phares, Samuel told the story of how someone offered to adopt Leah! This woman had only boys and thought having a little girl would be nice. The family was only marginally involved in the church, and Samuel had failed to persuade her to bring her youngest son to Sunday School. My gentle grandfather wrote, "Believe me, I closed my fist and said no with more emphasis than I ever put on that word."

How could this woman fail to understand that the family he and Fianna had created was now *his* to care for, that the children were *his* to love and guide and raise? They were a responsibility and a comfort. Through these little ones, he had something of Fianna to cherish.

Samuel also found comfort through the love of poetry that he and Fianna had shared. After Fianna's death, Samuel turned to their favorite poet Longfellow again. His sister-in-law Naomi recommended a few poems that might speak to him. Longfellow's first wife had died after only four years of marriage, and Longfellow wrote "Footsteps of Angels" about her. Samuel found particular comfort in that poem and referred to it in several letters:

Naomi, I read those poems from Longfellow and they mean so much more than when I read them at school. Doesn't he refer most beautifully to his Being Beauteous in "Footsteps of Angels", also in "Village Blacksmith" and in "Two Locks of Hair" he refers to both wife & child. His poem "The Reaper and the Flowers" written after the death of the child is certainly also rich. So is the "Psalm of Life." May I say to you all and to myself as he says in "The Rainy Day".

 Be still, sad heart! and cease repining,
 Behind the clouds is the sun still shining,
 Thy fate is the common fate of all,
 Into each life some rain must fall,
 Some days must be dark and dreary.

(May 3, 1915)

When Samuel wrote to Fianna's parents, he wrote of the comfort he found in Longfellow's expression of grief. Perhaps Fianna's parents read "Footsteps of Angels" and found comfort, too.

Naomi asked me to reread Longfellow's poem "Footsteps of Angels." Those words mean much more than they ever before meant to me.

 Some of my feelings are there put in words.

(May 2, 1915)

CHAPTER 22

A Year Passes

In the midst of grief, the ordinary events of daily life continued. Through Samuel's letters, I learned of big and little happenings as the seasons of that first year unfolded. They had a good harvest although the raspberries were destroyed by hail. The corn cutters came to harvest the corn. His brother Levi came to help harvest the cherries. There was a bank examination, and he had a lot of preparation to do. He was nervous about a talk he needed to give at a church meeting, and he was rehearsing at home.

The farm, his work at the bank, and church activities were constants in his life. His heart, however, was with his children and home. He wrote to his brother:

Thursday of last week it was three weeks that Ammon and I are alone. Hannah has rheumatism. This is lonesome but I don't want <u>anybody</u> in the house. I want to take care of my name and of Ammon and of the household goods . . .
(Aug. 1, 1915)

It was a few months until he found another housekeeper. Samuel assured Mary that they were managing without Hannah and described their day:

Our daily program consists of something like this. Rise at 4:00 to 4:30. Feed stock, milk, take cows to pasture, prepare breakfast by this time Ammon usually gets awake and comes down. Then we have morning worship and breakfast, wash dishes, prepare for bank, and Ammon goes along as far as Grandma Meyer's where he stays until I come back. I have been taking supper there every evening so far except last evening when I didn't fetch Ammon until after teacher training. I don't write this to draw on your sympathy but I know you are anxious to know how we get along. If we are well we can get along this way.

(July 11, 1915)

Little Ammon kept things lively and delighted his father. Samuel must have chuckled when he saw Ammon standing in the barnyard "like a little man with his straw hat on the back of his head and both his hands propped on his hips firing questions at me." In another letter, he told how Ammon's new suit had arrived, and he had taken his son to have a haircut. Ammon looked "a picture" in his velvet suit and barbered hair. How much he longed to share such moments with Fianna, wishing that she could have seen how the young boy was growing.

At Christmas they made a trip to the Bucher family, and saw little Leah. Did she know that this man was her father and that Ammon was her brother? She was two years old, growing strong and talking much more than when he had seen her last. Early in the New Year, however, she gave them a real scare. She was very sick, and Mary was afraid it was tuberculosis!

Samuel wrote back to Mary:

I am glad you write so frankly . . . You have not yet been able to convince me that Leah has tuberculosis and I don't think you wanted to either. Leah was so well and strong and to drop in one day and be a sickly child, that I don't think is the way tuberculosis works.

. . . We are hoping that it will not come to this. I know that she is very well taken care of. I wish I could be with her oftener . . .

(Jan. 6, 1916)

Samuel yearned to see his little daughter and to care for her himself. He knew that he couldn't take care of two small children, his farm, and his work at the bank.

Leah and Ammon Meyer, 1914

Samuel was also called to work within the church. He was particularly drawn to Sunday School work. Sunday School was held on Sunday afternoon or evening as an outreach to the community. Children from the local area were invited, even if their parents did not attend church. Samuel loved to teach the primary class, and his class had grown large.

He sent Mary and Phares a copy of the request he made that the church would organize a Sunday School at another meetinghouse where the congregation held worship services. He concluded his request with:

> ... you may think this request does not come from the right source but you all know that if the farmer does not sow his field until the field asks for the seed, then the sowing will never be done.
>
> (Nov. 26, 1915)

I hope they accepted his proposal. I'm sure his sense of humor drew the children to him in his classes, and I hope it also worked with the adults who would decide whether to open a second Sunday School.

However, church work was not without strife. When planning for a regional conference about Sunday School work, Samuel met with "a stubborn committee" and wrote Mary about it:

> We never yet had any sisters on the program and the paper I presented to the church at the August council allowed this. I did not yield my ground on that point but on a few others which I am afraid will spoil our programs.
>
> (Sept. 12, 1915)

I am delighted that my grandfather "did not yield" on this issue. For Brethren of that era, including women in program leadership was controversial. I believe that knowing and loving Fianna influenced him. Perhaps he imagined her presenting at such a program, and he wanted to open the door for other women.

A few months later, Samuel wrote to Mary that he was going to be asked to be Sunday School superintendent. He dreaded this responsibility:

> *Fianna . . . often said she pities the man who will be our present Sunday School superintendent's successor. <u>Now I am alone</u> and father told me yesterday that the council will lay that all on me. The souls of the children of this community are the burden of my heart or I would absolutely refuse. I am afraid I don't have righteousness enough to face the devil when he comes in the person of false Brethren.*
>
> (Dec. 20, 1915)

Although I don't know the church struggles he referred to, I know that my childhood church community, the same one Samuel served, included a few inflexible members for whom a self-righteous love of power outweighed the community's welfare.

Samuel served briefly as Sunday School superintendent, but soon other church responsibilities came to him. A year after Fianna's death, Samuel was called by the congregation to become one of its ministers. At this time, ministry, like other church work, was unpaid and part-time. Each congregation had several men who shared the work. Ministry differed from other church commitments, however, because a minister served for the rest of his life.

Many years later when Samuel died, his college roommate Howard Merkey wrote a letter of sympathy to my parents and told what happened when Samuel was chosen:

> . . . the announcement was made that Samuel Meyer was the choice of the church, he rushed out of the sanctuary and sat in his team until some one went after him and brought him in.
>
> (May 29, 1969)

I wonder what Samuel thought as he sat alone in the buggy. He must have longed for Fianna. He wished that she could be with him to share this burden and responsibility as it would unfold through the rest of his life. This strong, thoughtful man was rightly chosen as minister. His gentle faithfulness would serve the church well, but he surely needed Fianna by his side. The "split trunk" was not healed even though new growth had begun around the wound.

This Is My Grandmother

During the months I read Fianna's letters and papers, discovering the world in which she lived and who she was in that world, I learned to know her.

Sometimes I felt I was truly there with her. I could almost hear her voice speaking to Samuel or her children. I was present as she wept for the loss of Baby Rufus and while she talked together with her college friends. I watched while she worked hard to clean and cook and sew as a young homemaker, then go out to the barn to feed the animals, and return to the house to care for Ammon and Leah. I watched silently as she slept on the White Haven balcony while snowflakes fell upon her, and I stood by her bedside with Samuel and her parents as she lay dying.

No, I never actually met my grandmother Fianna—but I am sure I'd know her if she walked into my study today. Sometimes, when I was reading her letters and the accounts written about her, I half-expected her to show up. Her strength and spirit would have been comforting because, as I wrote this story, I grieved her loss and wept along with Samuel and the family.

I never met her, but I can describe her. A slender, dark-haired woman, graceful and smiling, she had a tender heart and a ready interest in others. She kept in touch with old school friends.

At White Haven, she shared her delight at the beautiful dress sister Mary made for Leah with the other patients, and she wrote a letter for her illiterate Polish roommate. She had a lively sense of fun to match Samuel's. "Whatever you do, don't keep Samuel!"

Growing up within the large Bucher clan was formative for Fianna. Being a Bucher gave her church and family connections almost anywhere she went. She missed that family closeness when she married Samuel. When she was dying, she and Samuel talked about the future. She was particularly concerned that Samuel and the children would still belong among the Buchers after she was gone.

Even as Fianna's strength was failing, she longed to do the work of homemaking and mothering. Her older siblings had established their homes and families, and she had looked forward to the same flowering in her life with her beloved Samuel. I cannot imagine how painful it was to let go, to accept "God's will."

Fianna was a woman of strong faith. She lived within a community that did not question God's will even though they might struggle to accept it. She lived within a faith that could pray for healing and believe a loving God could heal—and yet accept that it might not be God's will to heal although they could not understand it. Her faith strengthened her to bear witness in the White Haven world that was so strange to her. She couldn't accept stolen toast. She remained pleasant and cheerful even when those around her habitually complained. And she spoke out firmly when she felt the staff mistreated her. Her faith gave her courage.

Fianna's faith gave her hope, too. She knew there was life with the "Heavenly Father" beyond this earthly life. She comforted Samuel with the words "I'll wait for you on the other side." Ammon was told about this promise when he was a child. And when he was dying, and I sat by his bedside, Ammon told me. He told me that he didn't understand how it could be true but he believed it anyway. Her faith strengthened his faith.

Fianna never stopped giving thanks for all that was done for her—the gentle ministrations of Leah, the presence of Samuel, Mary's care for little Dolly, the prayers of the people who loved her. The cheerful spirit that brought Dr. Weiss to tears remained strong until she died. This was the heart of who she was.

In my turn, I have been grateful for these months of reading old letters and writing this story, uncovering the grandmother I never knew. I am grateful to those who saved the papers so that finally, a century after they were written, I could be introduced to her, follow her through her life, and learn to know her and love her.

Grandmother, your life has spoken to me and blessed me.

What Happened to Them Later?

SAMUEL

Samuel remarried a year and a half after Fianna's death. He married Elizabeth Miller, a woman of the local church congregation who had trained as a teacher. In a letter to Mary and Phares, Samuel wrote that if a widower remarried within a few years, people were likely to say, "Now he's already forgotten his first wife." He emphatically denied that could ever happen:

Let me tell you with all the force at my command that that expression is not always true. When two souls lived together like Fianna and I did (until two souls become one soul) then there is no forgetting. I don't even know whether I can ever be happily married again. When one has had such a sweet better half the possibilities are great to make a failure of married life. I need your prayers more for the children's sake than for my own in order to do the right things.

(Aug. 20, 1915)

No, Samuel had not forgotten Fianna in a year and a half. But, he was determined to rebuild his life and have his family together again, and Elizabeth was a good woman and a good companion. If he wasn't as much in love as he had been with Fianna, he believed love would grow in the marriage. And so it did. Samuel and Elizabeth were married for over 50 years and had six children together. They died six weeks apart, and Samuel is buried between Fianna and Elizabeth.

In 1918, after seven years working at the bank, Samuel returned to teaching. Since he taught in the local one-room school, he taught some of his own children. He also continued to farm. I remember visiting the barn when I was a small child and watching the chickens scrabbling in the dirt and clucking noisily.

My memories of Grandpa Meyer center on holidays and special family gatherings when we would gather with others at their home. In this large group, he sat quietly watching his grandchildren play on the floor and smiling to himself, or he sat at the table as all the adult women bustled around serving an enormous holiday dinner.

With eight children, the table had to be a big one. And, with eight children, Samuel struggled to support his family. Teachers' salaries were small and farming was not profitable during the Depression. He could do little to help his children with college costs. However, through scholarships and borrowing and supporting each other, six of them graduated from college—Elizabethtown College, of course.

Teaching and farming provided an income but Samuel's first calling was ministry and church work. He preached throughout eastern Pennsylvania, frequently every evening for two weeks in evangelistic services. He was invited to work with churches on Christian education and missions, and sometimes he served as congregational moderator. He helped to organize the first Vacation Bible School that his congregation offered to the community. He always had a heart for children.

After a few years, Samuel took on the heavy responsibility of serving his congregation as presiding elder, the unpaid minister in charge of organizing all the ministry work of a congregation with half a dozen locations where services were held. For 17 years he served in this role, always available for problem solving and often receiving criticism. Members were sometimes fiercely loyal to a specific worship site rather than to the congregation as a whole. This was hard work but he knew he was called to it; it was his work for God.

LEAH

Leah lived "to be a good little woman," as her mother's postcard wished for her. Until she was four, she lived with Mary and Phares, and she remained strongly attached to them. Every summer she spent weeks of summer vacation there. I wonder what her life at home with her Papa and stepmother was like. What happened to that lively little girl as she grew up, the oldest girl in a family of six brothers and one little sister? I think she was put to work! In her high school yearbook, she is described as a quiet, serious book-lover.

After finishing high school, Leah worked five years as a housekeeper for a wealthy Lebanon family to earn money for college. Like many others, she worked a term, and then attended school a term, until she finally graduated when she was almost 30.

Leah became a teacher. She began with a one-room school, and then she taught first grade in the same classroom for over 30 years. Living and working near Philadelphia, she found a nearby church community that welcomed her and made her feel at home.

Leah never married. I have often wondered if she had any suitors, if she refused any proposals. I remember visiting her apartment when I was a child, and how she bustled around to serve us dinner. When she was older, my parents kept a room for her in their home, a space to be with family when she visited the community where she grew up. She was a delightful aunt, always interested in my brother and me.

AMMON

Ammon is my father. I know most about him, but I don't know what growing up in a household bustling with younger brothers was like for Ammon. The six-year gap between Ammon and his next younger brother meant Ammon was always in a different stage of childhood. I imagine Ammon standing a little separate and lonely while that restless pack of energetic little brothers frolicked.

Although he had no money, Ammon was determined to get a college education. He and his brother Nathan worked on neighboring farms and painted houses to earn tuition money. He graduated from Elizabethtown College with debts and few job prospects. Among his papers, I found a note written by a local school official giving him advance notice of a teaching position in a one-room school. He applied and was accepted.

Ammon had prepared to teach high school science and math, but he could only find work within elementary schools. So he sensibly focused on that which was within reach. When he could financially afford it, he returned to school and earned a graduate degree in elementary education administration from Temple University.

Ammon eventually became an elementary school principal at the Linglestown Elementary School near Harrisburg. In Ammon's school, there was a warm, supportive environment where teachers and principal worked together as a team. His gentle leadership, his respect for both teachers and students, and his organizational gifts brought him respect and love. His teacher friends stayed in touch with him for the rest of his life.

The same year Ammon began his teaching career, his congregation called him to the ministry. He was 23 years old. He would, as he sometimes said with a chuckle, "never again lack for something to do."

Ammon married Lucille Wenger whose family was as deeply rooted in this congregation as his was. He had known her his whole life, and they married a month after she graduated from Elizabethtown College. Their wedding, the first held in church rather than the bride's home, followed immediately after the Sunday morning service. They invited the whole congregation!

Not only did Ammon follow in the footsteps of his minister and teacher forebears but he also took on a family farm, not his father's or grandfather's, but his great-grandparents' farm, the Gibbel farm. He bought it from an uncle, and my brother Luke and I grew up there. Lucille's parents also lived on the farm, and everyone worked together in field and garden during the summer school break.

If Ammon wasn't farming and teaching, he was carrying out the work of ministry. He, like his father, became presiding elder of his church. He, also like his father, carried the burden of a divided congregation—divided in loyalty to church buildings and divided in theology. In spite of many patient efforts to create solutions and build bridges, some members eventually withdrew their membership. I was an adolescent then, and I remember how heartbreaking this was for him. He continued to minister to the congregation, however, and was able to prepare them for a paid pastor.

In retirement, he and Lucille entered Brethren Volunteer Service and served other churches as pastoral associates. It was tremendously fulfilling for them to use their gifts in new settings.

ACKNOWLEDGEMENTS

I am deeply grateful for the encouragement and assistance I received as I wrote *Fianna's Story*. I remember floating around the Galapagos Islands and watching my daughters, Diana and Alisa, and sister-in-law Doreen use precious holiday time to read and comment on the manuscript. A hearty thank you! Thank you also to Pat Reed and Pat Moore for their careful reading of the manuscript, and to Butch Reigart for his aid in translating Pennsylvania German into English. I am deeply grateful to Dolores Parsil whose encouragement and amazing editorial aid helped this book become a reality. Finally, my greatest gratitude goes to my husband Larry. Without his patient listening and loving support, I would never have completed this project.

If my ancestors had not been savers, there would be no story, and the richness of this woman's life could not be shared. Neither you nor I would know Fianna. Fianna's parents, siblings, and husband kept the letters they received and passed them on. They eventually came to Fianna's children, Ammon and Leah, and finally to me. Now her story belongs to all of us.

About the Author

NANCY L. BIEBER enjoys exploring her family's history through researching genealogy and uncovering treasures in her attic. Nancy calls *Fianna's Story* her "accidental book." "I didn't plan to write a book about Fianna," she said. "I simply wanted to share her amazing story with her descendants so I began to write!"

Nancy is a psychologist, teacher, and spiritual director. She is the author of *Decision Making & Spiritual Discernment* (SkyLight Paths) and often leads spiritual retreats within the United States and abroad. She lives in rural Lancaster County (PA) with her husband Larry. Together they enjoy gardening, traveling to explore the world's wonders, and spending time with their family.

To learn more about Nancy or to contact her, visit:
www.nancybieber.com